A Fine and Priv

Jesmond Old Cemetery, Newcastle upon Tyne

Alan Morgan

Or should I long, in sorrow's chillness,
To muse among the silent dead
Thy cemetery's mural stillness
Shall tempt my soft and pensive tread.

James Horsley: 'Jesmond, a Poem'

Tyne Bridge Publishing

The headstone detail on the back cover commemorates Matthew Charlton (died 1852) and family of Jesmond. The front cover photograph shows the memorial to Archibald Reed.

Acknowledgments:

The author and Tyne Bridge Publishing would like to thank the following: Sally Bird, Jimmy Donald, Anthony Flowers, Tim Flowers, Dave Heslop, Stafford Linsley, John Nolan, Lynn Redhead, Bob Rennison, Steve Speak, Olive Taylor, Lawrence Truman, Ronnie Tweedy, Tom Yellowley, the Friends of Jesmond Dene, the Local Studies Section at Newcastle City Library, Tyne & Wear Archives.

Tyne Bridge Publishing would like to thank Strettle of Newcastle Ltd. for their generous support.

Also by Alan Morgan: Bygone Jesmond Dene, Bygone Shieldfield, Bygone Jesmond Vale, Bygone Sandyford and Cradlewell, Bygone Lower Ouseburn, all published by Newcastle Libraries.

For those intending to visit Jesmond Old Cemetery, opening times are:

October - March

Mon -Thurs	8.00am - 3.45pm	
Fri	8.00am - 2.45pm	
Sat, Sun, Bank Holidays	11.00am - 3.45pm	

April - September

Mon-Fri	8.00am - 6.45pm
Sat, Sun, Bank Holidays	11.00am - 4.45pm

ISBN: 1 85795 155 7

Tyne Bridge Publishing, City of Newcastle upon Tyne, Education & Libraries Directorate
Newcastle Libraries & Information Service, 2000

Printed by Bailes the Printer, Houghton-le-Spring

Contents

Dust to Dust: an Introduction to Jesmond Old Cemetery

eath comes to us all, and each human society commemorates the dead in its own way. By the early 1800s the question of where to put mortal remains so the deceased might be remembered with dignity had become a practical problem in urban Britain. Newcastle's citizens found a handsome solution.

By the early years of the 19th century most people had long had the legal right to be buried in their parish churchyard. Many urban churchyards became grossly overcrowded and 'an affront to public decency' and Church of England ministers, who had a certain interest in the collection of burial fees, made little objection. Alternative burial grounds were comparatively rare partly owing to the cost and the inconvenience of having to travel away from the local church. Even space for burials within a church, usually reserved for the rich and well-to-do, had reached saturation point and were considered a nuisance as well as an unhealthy practice. Cremation was not to become an option until the late 19th century when the first crematorium in the UK opened in Woking in 1885.

As early as the 17th century Christopher Wren, the architect of St Paul's Cathedral in London, had floated the idea of locating cemeteries outside town walls, but his suggestions were not taken up. An exception was the establishment of burial grounds by some of the dissenting religions, such as the Quakers, in order to avoid the statutory Anglican burial service within a parish churchyard where no non-conformist minister could officiate. The remains of just such an alternative to the overcrowded parish churchyards can be seen today at Ballast Hills near the Lower Ouseburn, once the largest dissenters' burial ground near Newcastle.

As the population increased burials had to be crammed into relatively small and often shrinking churchyards. Corpses rarely lay undisturbed for long before their bones were lifted to make way for new interments. Bones were usually stored in a charnel house in the church. This procedure occurred in Newcastle at St Nicholas' church (it did not become a cathedral until 1882) where a charnel house once existed in what is now the crypt. When it was cleared in 1824 'it was found nearly filled with human bones, the larger ones in regular piles'.

Another way of accommodating further coffins was to introduce fresh soil to create more depth and this is why today many churchyards appear to rise above the surrounding pavement levels, and the entrance to the church often appears to be sunken.

Further problems arose in parish churchyards in the mid 18th century. As the demand for fresh corpses from the medical schools often outstripped supply from legitimate sources body snatching became a common and profitable activity. Access to churchyards was relatively easy and graves were becoming increasingly shallow. The teeth of the deceased could also be a valuable commodity.

By the 19th century the health risk arising from overcrowding had become another issue and it is on record that clergy officiating at funerals in parish churchyards often carried earth in their pockets for scattering onto the coffin so they would not have to pick up contaminated soil. In 1832 two grave diggers in Aldgate in London died as a result of inhaling foul air. Many churches were close to streams and before the days of piped water, disease was a continual threat. In fact it was the outbreak of cholera in the 1850s that finally closed all town parish churchyards in Newcastle (and elsewhere in England) in favour of suburban cemeteries.

In the 1820s a movement began, for those who could afford it, for out-of-town private cemeteries in quiet and attractive surroundings. Here bodies could remain undisturbed for ever

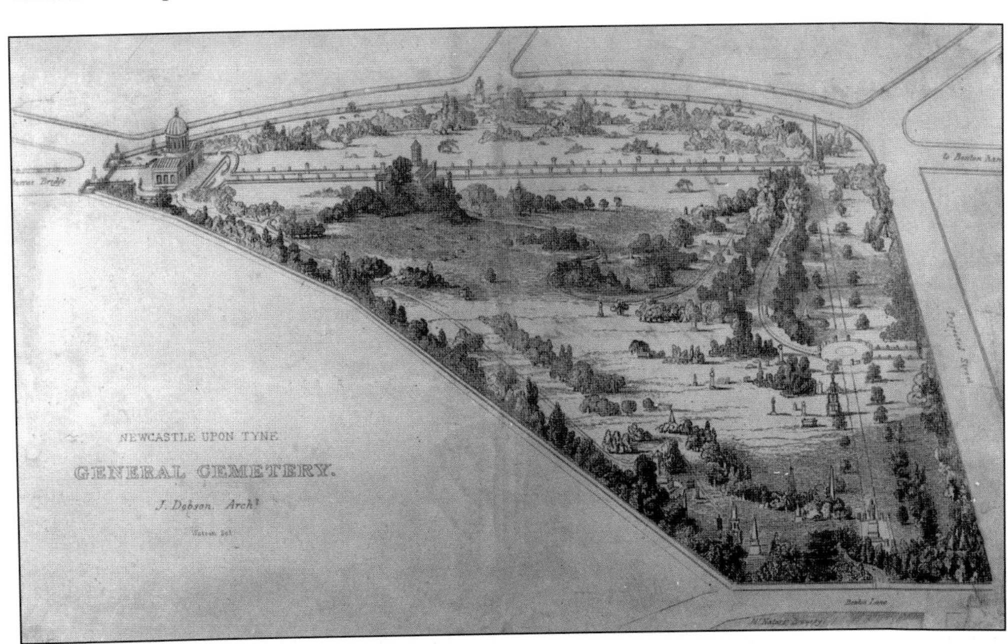

Tyne & Wear Archives

The Newcastle General Cemetery as envisioned by John Dobson in the 1830s. The concept, with its mausoleum, was much grander than the final design.

(it was thought) in a chosen plot, access was limited, burial services could be conducted in a calm and dignified manner (town churchyards tended to be noisy and irreverent). There was relative security from the 'resurrection men' behind the high surrounding walls and gates were locked at dusk. Most importantly for the Victorian middle classes, they could be seen to be buried with others of a similar social status.

The idea seems to have originated in Paris though earlier examples were known in Calcutta, Edinburgh and Belfast. Newcastle was one of the earliest English towns to follow the trend when in 1829 Westgate Hill Cemetery was opened 'to the whole human family without difference or distinction'. Norwich had been the first inter-denominational cemetery in England in 1819 followed by similar establishments in Liverpool, Cheltenham, London, and Birmingham before the opening in 1836 of Newcastle General Cemetery. The last of these private cemeteries was set up in the 1850s by which time the urban churchyards had been replaced by the familiar Municipal Cemeteries we know today.

In 1833 the Mayor of Newcastle, Henry Bell, was requested by many of the town's leading citizens including John Dobson, architect, and Richard Grainger, property developer, to call a meeting 'to form and establish, for the use of the town, a General Cemetery a measure for which the crowded state of the church yards had long rendered necessary'.

John Dobson's magnificent entrance arch, Jesmond Road.

The meeting was held in the Guildhall early in 1834 and it was agreed to form a private company to carry out the scheme with a share capital of £8,000 (400 shares of £20) which was considered enough to cover purchase of the ground plus the necessary building and landscaping work. A Prospectus was issued inviting subscribers for shares and adding that the proposed cemetery would be on 11 acres in Jesmond Fields, owned by the Corporation, surrounded by cornfields

Newcastle General Cemetery, as it was known then, in the 1840s.

and meadows. The cemetery would be open to all religious denominations, roughly one half as consecrated ground to be ministered by the curate of St Andrew's, in whose parish the cemetery would lie, and the other half as unconsecrated ground for all non-conformists.

Investors would be attracted by the fact that a freehold plot could be sold without buyers fearing disturbance, and the added revenue from sales of family vaults and catacombs meant that a healthy dividend return would be likely. These family vaults were to be brick-lined with stone shelves supported on corbels to carry the lead-lined coffins. They could be as deep as six metres and were popular because coffins survived longer when not in contact with soil. Another incentive to shareholders was their automatic entitlement to a County vote at the elections.

John Dobson was appointed architect. Work began in 1835 when the land was drained, three-metre walls erected to enclose the triangular site, and construction got under way. During the following year a sexton-gardener was appointed at 18 shillings a week, with free accommodation and coal, and he assisted the architect in the laying out of the serpentine paths and the planting of trees and shrubs.

John Dobson's achievement is impressive. The main entrance from Cemetery Road (now Jesmond Road) has a huge arch surmounted by two square towers. On either side were the two chapels, Church of England to the west and non-conformist to the east, in local sandstone ash-

lar, built in the classical Grecian style. The imposing entrance leaves no doubt that this is the gateway to a solemn place, no public park or country house. The buildings also contained accommodation for the resident cemetery superintendent and his office for books and registers. Beneath the buildings were the catacombs, 22 large shelved enclosures identified by Roman numerals. They were, like vaults below churches, designed for the permanent storage of compulsory lead-lined (air-tight) coffins. However, there seems to be no evidence that they were used as such and they probably functioned as mortuary vaults to store coffins before burial at a time when funeral parlours were much rarer than today. It may be that the catacombs were used during World War Two as temporary accommodation for victims of a local air raid.

Today the Archaeology Department of Tyne and Wear Museums and the County Archaeologist occupy the buildings and store equipment in the catacombs.

At the south side of the cemetery on Benton Lane (now Sandyford Road) was a single storey lodge (now disused) for the sexton, standing beside massive square sandstone gate pillars, again in the Grecian style, with iron gates.

The high wall surrounding the cemetery was built to deter bodysnatchers and is very different from the railings and low wall of All Saints Cemetery opposite, built some 20 years later. By that time the 1832 Anatomy Act, which stated that medical schools could use any unclaimed corpses (not just criminals) once 48 hours had elapsed, had put most bodysnatchers out of work.

The western half of the cemetery was consecrated by the Bishop of Durham on 11th November 1836 and declared open for burials five days later. On 9th December Margaret Redford Hoy, the 14-year-old daughter of a Newcastle grocer, was the first to be buried in the cemetery. Her grave, in the non-conformist section, was unmarked.

By 1845 non-conformist family vaults near the Middle Walk were not selling as well as had been expected so this land too was consecrated by the Bishop of Durham.

The cemetery went on fulfilling its function undisturbed for well over a century. It escaped serious damage during World War II but a few headstones to the east side of the Middle Walk are said to have been hit by enemy aircraft fire.

However, in the mid 1960s plans were prepared for a dual carriageway to connect the Coast Road from Tynemouth with the Central Motorway East along a widened Jesmond Road. This inevitably meant encroaching on part of the cemetery, and in 1967 the private company was wound up and returned to the City Council. The proposed upheaval would involve major problems – about 600 graves (nearly 1,100 burials) some more than 100 years old, would need to be

One of the bullet-damaged grave stones.

City Repro

Re-interment following the upheavals of 1971. This obelisk belongs to the Patrick Freeman family.

exhumed and reinterred, and John Dobson's magnificent entrance gateway and chapels would have to be moved.

The legal machinery whirred into action. Notices were issued and attempts made to contact relatives of all those burials involved. Relatives were then given the right to carry out removals to any other cemetery, up to a maximum cost of £100, or allow a transfer to another part of the cemetery. The Council undertook to re-erect all monuments and tombstones unless in a ruinous condition. Years later the number of unclaimed graves was 'considerable', and of those families successfully contacted only two opted for private removal. Only one was 'not keen to have remains disturbed'. The rest of the tombs had to be moved without consent.

The estimated cost of re-siting the gateway and chapels amounted to £100,000. This

seemed too expensive to the City Planning Department and demolition was proposed. However, pressure from conservation groups brought the Environment Minister into the controversy. Because the buildings were of exceptional architectural and historical importance, as well as being structurally sound, dry-jointed and capable of being re-erected elsewhere, he offered a 75 per cent grant. Suggestions for the new site included Leazes Park, Denton Burn Crematorium, a new entrance to All Saints Cemetery at the east end of Clayton Road, and replacing the gateway on Sandyford Road. Other plans involved making them into a symbolic gateway to the city at the eastern tip of Jesmond Old Cemetery, or just moving everything 40 metres into the cemetery, necessitating the transfer of even more graves. The problem was rapidly becoming a test case of national importance as at this time no historic building had ever been officially wiped out by a motorway.

In 1971 work began on the removal of the graves, 'with the utmost reverence' by the London Necropolis Company, and although they usually carried out exhumations at night constraints on this project meant that they worked in daylight too with protective screening. Public access was not allowed. All soil was sifted for remains which were then re-coffined and reburied. The work on the Jesmond Road border took several months and at a later date more

Like Highgate Cemetery in London Jesmond Old Cemetery has become a wilderness of tombs.

exhumations took place on the Sandyford Road side and in the South West area. Eventually the whole Bypass scheme collapsed because of legal difficulties and when the project was resurrected nearly 30 years later the 'dualling' of Jesmond Road and the widening of Sandyford Road never took place.

Burials are still taking place in the cemetery and at the last count nearly 25,000 people have been buried there since 1836. The first investors might have been concerned to find that today plots may not be bought in perpetuity, and are only leased for 50 years. Not all the graves are marked by a monument or a headstone. Although the grassed areas of the cemetery are mown regularly many parts have become jungles of vegetation with headstones and monuments submerged beneath a sea of brambles and ivy. Others have been damaged by self seeded saplings and falling trees. Such neglect could ultimately prove disastrous for this unique area of social history.

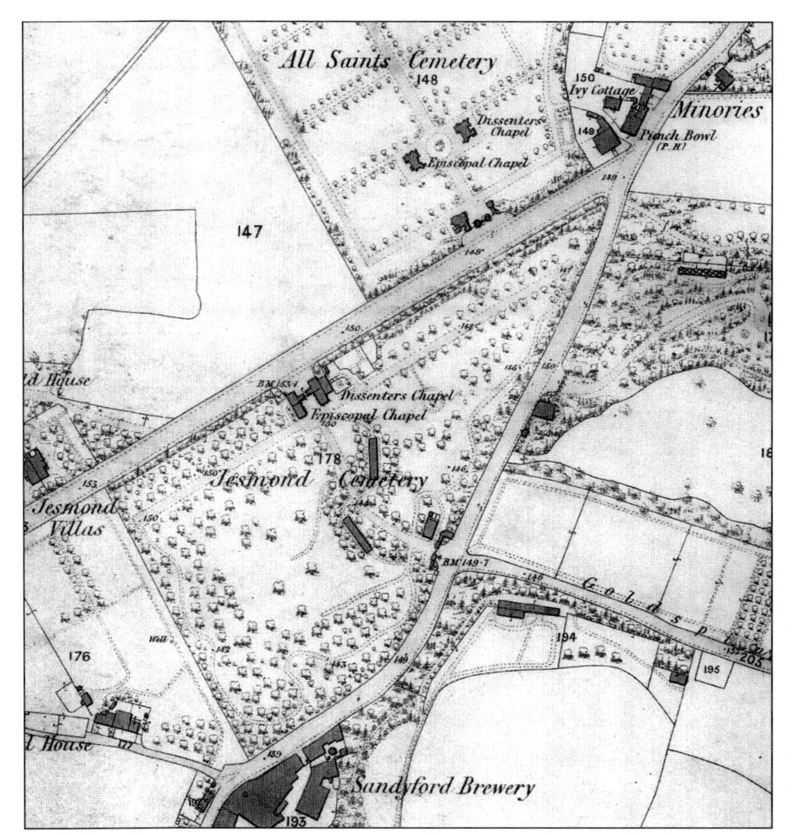

The rural setting of Jesmond Cemetery c.1859, before the development of Sandyford and Jesmond. All Saints Cemetery was opened in 1856.

RITES AND RITUALS

'But there, everything has its drawbacks, as the man said when his mother-in-law died and they came down on him for the funeral expenses.'

(Jerome K. Jerome, Three Men in a Boat, 1889)

In any society death rituals provide comfort for the bereaved. Elaborate funerals and the provision of a fitting memorial were a way in which the 19th century middle classes coped with the shock and unhappiness of bereavement. The advent of modern medicine has made death in childbirth and the death of infants much less frequent – if no less distressing – and diseases like cholera and typhoid are unlikely to see off the residents of urban England. The regularity with which many Victorian families had to deal with untimely death meant that bereavement was an experience to be accepted stoically. The customs of mourning helped the survivors to weather the time of grieving. Funerals became more and more elaborate throughout the 19th century and Queen Victoria set the fashion for very lengthy and strict mourning after the death of Prince Albert in 1861.

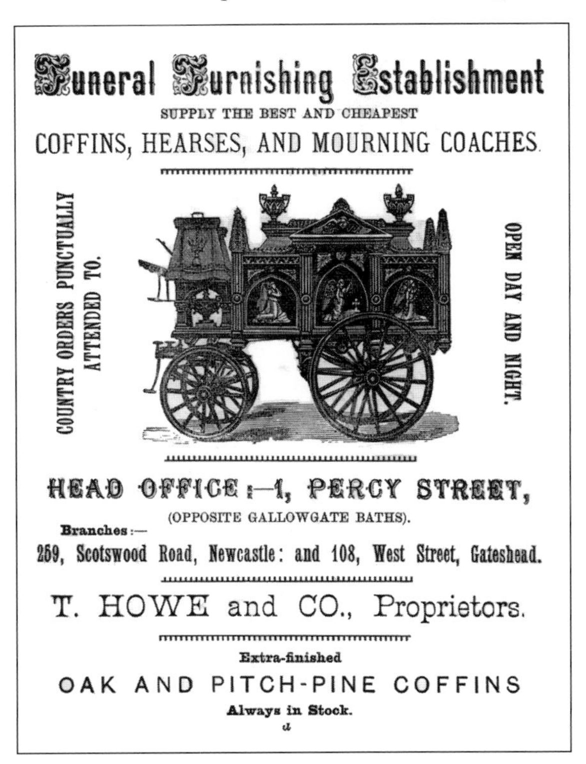

The name of T. Howe can still be seen high up on a building at the corner of Percy Street and Leazes Park Road.

From the time of death to the departure of the body for burial it was customary to keep all window blinds drawn, and this restriction might also include windows at the homes of relatives and neighbours. It was expected that the women of the family would not appear in public during this time. The corpse usually lay in the house, sometimes for up to two weeks, before bur-

CHARGES FOR INTERMENT			
Including every expense of the Ground and Registration; the Graves, in new Ground, Six Feet Deep			
	£	s.	d.
For a child under 10 years of age	0	5	0
For all above 10 years of age		7	6
For Permission to erect a Headstone at a Grave, or monumental pillar, not exceeding Two Feet Six Inches square	1	0	0
For Permission to cover the Grave by a flat Stone or Monument, or to surround it by Paling	3	0	0
If more than 6 feet deep extra 2/- per foot			

From the prospectus of the General Cemetery Company, 1834.

ial. This was often because there was insufficient cash available at death to pay for what might be expensive funeral arrangements, and because many funerals, particularly those of the working class, took place on Sundays – the one day of the week when work was not a priority.

By the mid-19th century burial costs (including fees but excluding any memorials) varied from around £1 10s for a labourer's child, up to nearly £1,500 for a titled person, and around £50-£60 for persons of 'moderate' respectability. A major item of expense in any funeral was the need for vast quantities of black material. Undertakers, to take care of all the business of the funeral, first appeared in London in the late 17th century and by Victorian times were advertising discreetly in trade directories and through trade cards. Anyone who could make a coffin could arrange a funeral and many joiners, builders and upholsterers provided undertaking as a sideline. The British Institute of Undertakers was formed in 1898. There was much exploitation by undertakers concerning coffins, hearses, horses, mutes and attendants – social status was an ever present preoccupation which Charles Dickens highlighted in this extract from *From the Raven in the Happy Family*:

'Undertaker: "Hearse and four, Sir?"

Client: "No a pair will be sufficient."

Undertaker: "I beg your par-

don, Sir, but when we buried Mr Grundy at No 20, there was four on 'em, Sir. I think it right to mention it."

Client: "Well perhaps there had better be four.'"

Costs thus escalated, in some cases leading to extravagance, bankruptcy and the application for 'poor law' relief. Dickens insisted in his will that his funeral should be carried out in 'an inexpensive, unostentatious and strictly private manner', and he wished mourners to 'wear no scarf, cloak, black bow, long hatband or other absurdity'.

All dreaded the stigma of a pauper's burial, and people scrimped and saved money they could barely afford against such a misfortune. Penny-a-week burial plans, provided by insurance and friendly societies, became increasingly popular as a way to ensure a sufficiently elaborate funeral on a limited income. Some funerals were carried out at night to avoid the 'show' aspect and so keep costs to a minimum. Savings would include avoiding the custom of having to give money and food to the poor at funerals and the cost of a sermon.

Another item of expense was the 'memorial card', edged in black and usually illustrated with angels, urns, and weeping willows, together with the name of the deceased. This was sent out to mourners after the funeral. Some are collectors' items today, particularly those of celebrities. The practice of edging in black anything else to do with the funeral, from newspaper announcements to the bereaved's writing paper and handkerchieves, meant further costs.

Mourning dress today is a rarity, but in Victorian times a widow was expected to be in deep

Family Mourning Department

The Stock in the Department embraces all the newest and most durable makes in Black Dress Fabrics. The following are a few of our Special Lots:—

	Ordinary Price.	Sale Price		Ordinary Price.	Sale Price
Black Heavy Serges	$6\frac{3}{4}$d	$4\frac{3}{4}$d	44 inch French Merinos	2/11	2/3
Black Wool Heavy Tweed	1/4$\frac{1}{2}$	$10\frac{3}{4}$d	44 inch French Merinos	4/9	3/6
Black Persian Cord	1/0$\frac{1}{2}$	$8\frac{3}{4}$d	44 inch Velvet Cashmere	2/11	2/1$\frac{1}{2}$
Black French Soft Serges	1/7$\frac{1}{2}$	1/0$\frac{1}{2}$	44 inch Velvet Cashmere	5/3	3/11
Black French Vicuna Cloth	1/9$\frac{1}{2}$	1/2$\frac{1}{2}$	Black Embroidered Robes	59/6	37/6
46 inch Habit Cloth	4/6	3/3	Black Plain and Checked Grenadines at Half Prices		

Funerals Furnished and Mourning Orders Executed with Despatch at Moderate Charges

Bainbridge's, as one of Newcastle's major department stores, had a Family Mourning Department to cater for the needs of bereaved families. This advertisement is from the catalogue of the 1888 bi-annual sale.

'A talk with a girlfriend who has to eschew colours during the summer led the present writer to ponder on the possibilities of looking cool and dainty even though obliged by the custom of society to wear mourning. It is to be sincerely hoped that these hints will not appeal to many, but to a few they may prove helpful … sketch shows a design for a more dressy frock in white muslin spotted with black.'

From *Newcastle Weekly Chronicle*, Saturday June 2nd 1906.

mourning for one year after the death of her husband, during which time her black clothes were usually made of worsted and cotton (which did not reflect the light). For the following six months she would wear black silk. After 18 months it was considered unlucky to wear or keep black crepe trimmings in the house. Following the second anniversary of death half mourning began when mauve or purple clothes were usually worn. Mourning jewellery, in black jet, was worn by wealthy women. A widow was not expected to socialise or remarry for the first year of deep mourning whereas a widower could take a wife immediately, provided they both wore mourning clothes for the official period of grief following their marriage. In addition to a black suit and tie, men wore black crepe bands around their hats or on their sleeves.

At the funeral itself, the deceased, became the focus of attention. Mutes, employed by undertakers, to solemnly and silently head the procession led the way from the house. Next would come the hearse, elaborately fitted out (glass-sided hearses first appeared in the 1860s) and pulled by a team of horses, often bedecked with attractive black plumes. It was the rise of the private cemeteries, distant from the local churchyard, that led to the use of these horse drawn hearses. Coffin bearers flanked the hearse as it progressed at a walking pace, and the mourning coaches followed. Attendants (black-clad men carrying paddles wrapped in black crepe) flanked the coaches. Empty coaches, suitably decked in mourning, would be sent by guests who could not come themselves. If the deceased was a military or civic dignitary his riding boots or weapons would be shown in the reverse position.

In the hearse would be the coffin covered with the pall – a cloth spread over the coffin. A

white edged pall was for a child, bachelor, spinster or woman who had died in childbirth. A black pall was for everyone else. The pall hung over the sides of the coffin as it was carried to the grave, covering the bearers to the waist, the edges being held by six mourners, dressed in either black or white and of similar status. The pall bearers also wore gloves, hatbands and silk scarves of the appropriate colour. Everyone carried a sprig of rosemary to be dropped into the grave on top of the coffin as a promise to the deceased that they would not be forgotten.

The coffin itself was sometimes quite elaborate and very costly. An obituary describes the coffin of one Bertram Brumell whose funeral in Jesmond Cemetery took place in 1905. 'The body was encased in poplar and lead shells, and these were placed in an outer oak coffin with brass mountings.' Chapman's, furniture makers, (see page 40) were agents for the Metallic Airtight Coffin Company.

After burial the choice of a fitting stone or memorial was most important. Some designed their own memorials before death, as in the case of Richard Cail in the North West cemetery, but there were a number of more conventional designs to choose from. Broken columns (signifying a life cut short), Greek urns, weeping angels, open bibles, obelisks, table tombs and Gothic script were all features of the Victorian cemetery. Before the 19th century monuments in the form of a cross were rarely used because of associations with Catholicism. Flat grave slabs (ledger stones) were a legacy from earlier times. Symbols such as that of the Freemasons, or describing occupations – for example a pen and palette for an artist, or an anchor and chain for a shipping firm, may also be seen in Jesmond Cemetery.

Some had a fear of being buried alive and stipulated in their wills that an artery was to be

A funeral procession enters Jesmond Cemetery around 1850, the funeral director leading the way.

Emley's monumental showrooms on Neville Street in the 1880s. They claimed to display 'one of the most artistic stocks' in the North.

severed. In one case there was a demand that the head should be severed and the heart extracted. Others simply requested there should be a two-week wait before burial. The cemeteries of continental Europe boasted intricate devices to allow a mistakenly buried person to summon assistance, should he or she revive. In one case, in Norfolk, a man was buried upright within an eight-foot pedestal above ground, thus ensuring he would not be trodden on.

ECONOMY UNITED WITH RESPECTABILITY & PROPRIETY

IN THE PURCHASE OF FUNERAL ATTIRE, AT THE

NEWCASTLE MOURNING & FUNERAL WAREHOUSE,

17, GREY STREET, NEWCASTLE,

ESTABLISHED FOR THE EXCLUSIVE SALE OF MOURNING.

G. FOREMAN, Proprietor.

It is quite evident that the MOURNING WAREHOUSEMAN, requiring an exclusive class of goods, can command *exclusive terms* from the MANUFACTURER. This is the usage in all trade. Here is a *saving at the commencement.* He, moreover, combines several firms in his ONE ESTABLISHMENT, each of which firms, when separated, carry off a distinct and individual profit. He does not require you to go to the *mercer*—the *milliner*—the *undertaker*, &c.,—every one of whom will draw his separate gains from the private mourner. His business and office are to supply and undertake *all* that is required. He deals wholesale for his materials, so that he is able to furnish the *Mourner* at ONE HALF the PRICES not unusually paid on such occasions; or on the most moderate calculation, at a saving of ONE-FOURTH.

But the *economy* of an establishment solely devoted to Mourning is not its *only claim* to public attention. Its sale being *exclusive*, is *rapid;* so that it is constantly stocked with *all the newest fabrics and patterns produced* both by *British* and *Foreign* manufacturers.

It being the exclusive *business* of such an establishment to supply Mourning, the whole attention of its proprietor is devoted to that purpose, and he must, therefore, be the best qualified to do so with PROPRIETY and RESPECTABILITY, united with ECONOMY, PUNCTUALITY, and DESPATCH.

☞ This Establishment is constantly being replenished with everything new and fashionable, adapted to the various seasons.

THE CEMETERY PLAN

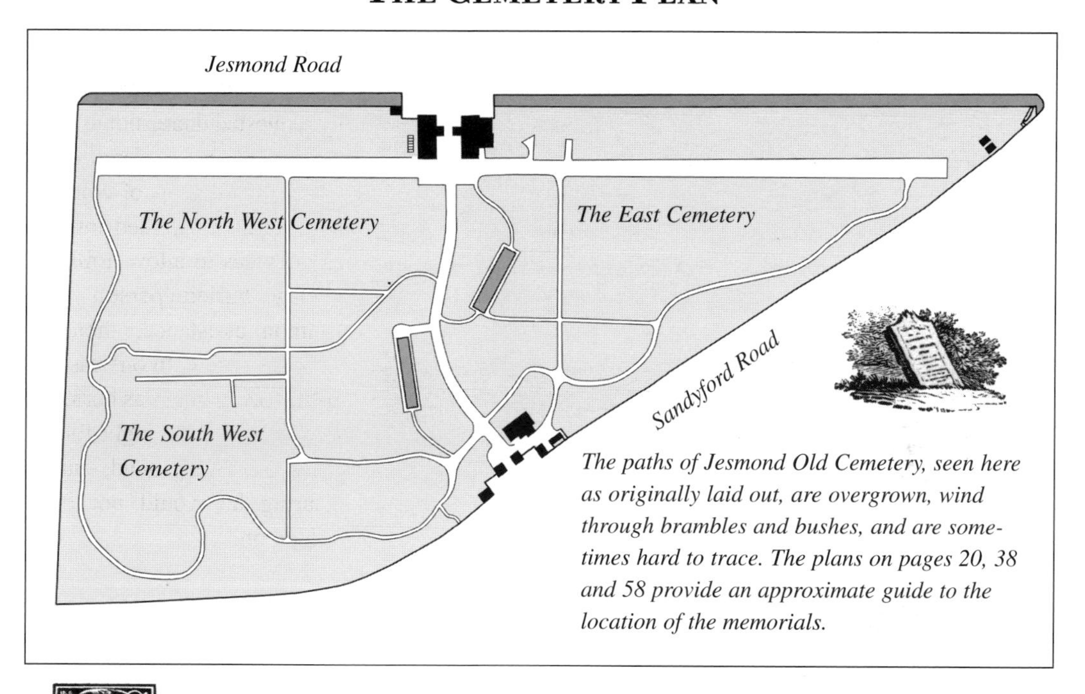

The paths of Jesmond Old Cemetery, seen here as originally laid out, are overgrown, wind through brambles and bushes, and are sometimes hard to trace. The plans on pages 20, 38 and 58 provide an approximate guide to the location of the memorials.

The cemetery may be divided into three sections – the North West, the South West and the East. A central path, the Middle Walk, crosses the cemetery.

Each section contains the memorials of men and women who were important to Newcastle's history in Victorian times and beyond. From the great architects John Dobson and Thomas Oliver to the familiar department store names of Bainbridge and Fenwick, many of the city's more famous inhabitants found their last resting place here. Less well known, but equally deserving of remembrance, are citizens from engineers to doctors who lie here too. There are graves which record the tragic deaths of wives in childbirth, and of whole strings of infants when infant mortality was rife. There are memorials to those who died violently, through crime or accident. And there are some magnificent examples of Victorian monumental sculpture.

In the sections which follow the most interesting graves and memorials in each area of the cemetery are described in alphabetical order, so that the reader may take an informed walk. For each section a detailed map with a key is provided.

The North West Cemetery

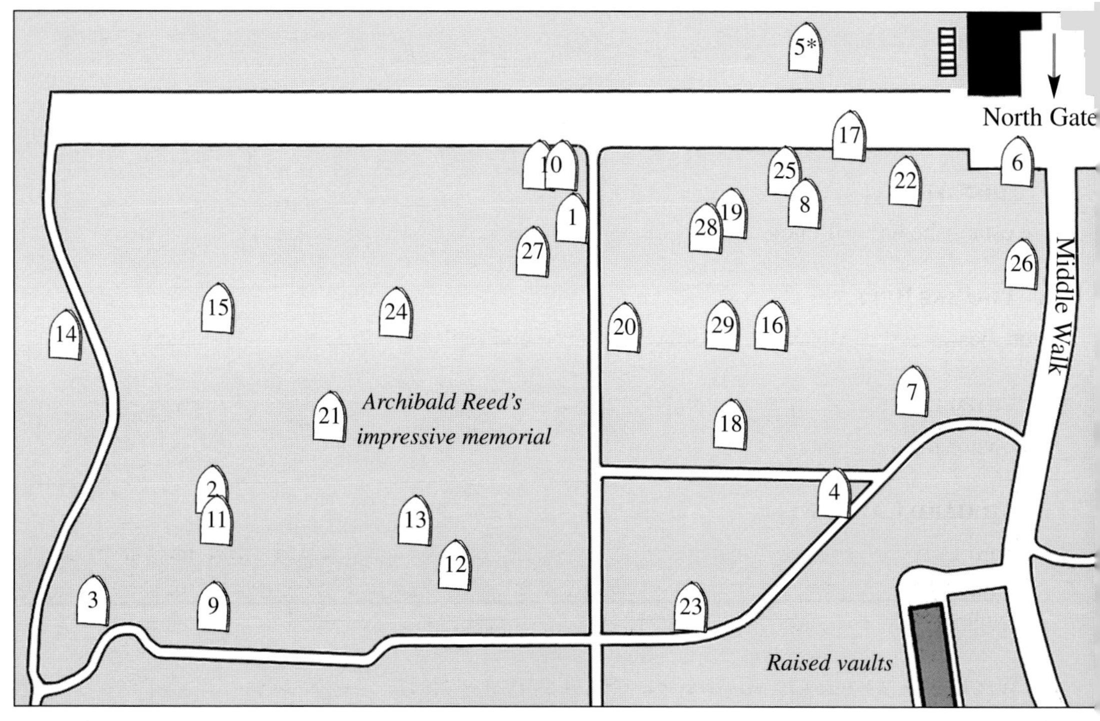

1. John Abbot
2. Thomas Bell
3. Thomas Lowe Bunting
4. Richard Cail
5. William Campbell *
6. Sid Chaplin
7. Abel Henry Chapman
8. John Dove
9. John Fleming
10. John Harvey, Herbert Davy
11. John Hawthorn
12. Alexander Laing
13. C. T. Maling
14. John Mawson
15. John Morrison
16. John Innes Nisbet
17. Jane Palmer
18. John Peter Parland
19. George Hare Philipson
20. William Rea
21. Archibald Reed
22. Thomas Miles Richardson
23. John Roach
24. William Spencer
25. Thomas Stokoe
26. John Cameron Swan
27. 'General' Terrot
28. John Humble Todd
29. Joe Wilson

* Unmarked grave

THE NORTH WEST CEMETERY

'Thou thy worldly task hath done,
Home art gone and ta'en thy wages'
Shakespeare, Cymbeline

1. JOHN ABBOT, 1784-1863. ENGINEER

He established a well-known firm of ironfounders and engineers in Gateshead.

2. THOMAS BELL, 1774-1845. IRON MASTER

Iron master at the Walker works of Losh, Wilson and Bell.

3. THOMAS LOWE BUNTING, 1868-1925. DOCTOR, FATHER OF BASIL BUNTING

Pit doctor for the Montague Colliery and father of the acclaimed poet Basil Bunting.

4. RICHARD CAIL, 1812-1893. BUILDING CONTRACTOR

Richard Cail specified his unusual massive four ton grey granite tombstone (reminiscent of a fallen tree trunk) in his will and designed it himself. He was much involved with railway and reservoir engineering, and was twice Mayor of Newcastle in 1872 and 1879.

5. WILLIAM CAMPBELL, 1856-1878. HEAVIEST MAN IN BRITAIN

Once the heaviest man in the country, the Scottish landlord of the Duke of Wellington on High Bridge is buried in an unmarked grave, and is famous for his enormous size. At his death aged 22 he weighed 53 stones and was 6 ft 3 ins tall. His chest measurement was 96 ins. The problem of the extraction of the huge coffin from the third floor of the public house provided a compelling attraction for the crowds. A specially constructed winch lowered the lead-lined box through the window, from which the frame and surrounding brickwork had been removed, and a black-draped horse-drawn lorry took the heavy load through the crowds. The streets were packed with sightseers estimated at 30,000-40,000. A brass band led the way. When the cortège arrived at Jesmond

Cemetery a local newspaper reported: 'a scene of most unseemly disorder ensued'. The band, while still playing the Dead March were 'rushed from their position and all that could be seen of them afterwards was a trumpet here and there frantically waving above the heads of the people'. The awful crush came near to injuring spectators at the gateway and inside the cemetery several were knocked into the grave. It took an hour's manoeuvring to get the coffin lowered. Apparently the grave was by the walk alongside the Jesmond Road wall, but no trace of it remains today.

6. SID CHAPLIN 1916-1986. WRITER

The son of a colliery electrician and the eldest of six children, Sid Chaplin was born at Shildon, County Durham. In mining areas it was assumed that most boys would eventually work in the local pit and in Sid's case he was employed at 14 in a local bakery until he began his apprenticeship as a colliery blacksmith. Fascinated by words, Sid wrote articles for the local newspaper between shifts in his early days at the pit but concealed his identity because literary leanings were not thought of as 'manly' at that time. As a young man he had been a Methodist lay preacher and aspired to a career in politics and economics.

His first publication in 1946 was a collection of short stories, *The Leaping Lad*, which won an award of £300 from the Rockefeller Trust. This enabled him to concentrate on writing for many months until the money ran out and he was forced back to the pit. In 1950 Sid joined the public relations department of the National Coal Board and moved to London as chief reporter for the mining magazine *Coal*. Returning to Newcastle several years later he wrote more books about working class life in the region, including *The Watchers and the Watched* and *The Day of the Sardine*. He became involved in the production of the musical play *Close the Coalhouse Door* and writing scripts for the television series *When the Boat Comes In*.

Retiring early from the NCB to work on his writing, Sid suffered a major heart attack in 1973. Four years later was awarded the OBE for services to the Arts in the North East where he had helped form Northern Arts in 1961. Sid is the only strictly 'non-Victorian' in this book.

7. ABEL HENRY CHAPMAN, 1836-1902, ENGINEER

First chairman of Gateshead engineering company of Clarke, Chapman & Co., est. 1864.

8. JOHN DOVE, 1789-1860. CEMENT MANUFACTURER

Founder of a cement manufacturing business at the Close, 1854.

9. JOHN FLEMING, 1807-1890. FOUNDER OF THE FLEMING MEMORIAL HOSPITAL FOR SICK CHILDREN

Solicitor who bequeathed over £100,000 to local charities including what became known as the Fleming Memorial Hospital for sick children.

10. JOHN HARVEY 1804-1893, HERBERT DAVY 1834-1889. TOBACCO KINGS

The 17th century French playwright, Molière, said 'There's nothing like tobacco: it is the passion of all decent men; a man who lives without tobacco does not deserve to live.' These words must have been music to the ears of John Harvey senior when in 1762 he opened a tobacconist's business at the sign of the Black Boy, head of Side, Newcastle. His widow moved the business to nearby larger premises 21 years later, and by 1856 this shop was also proving too cramped for the booming tobacco trade. Their grandson, John Harvey, moved the firm to Hanover Square where, with subsequent extensions and enlargements, it became the illustrated conglomeration of buildings.

HANOVER TOBACCO FACTORY.

The factory in Hanover Square in the 1880s.

About 300 women and girls were employed in the manufacture of various brands of which 'Brown Twist' was regarded as the favourite 'delicious smoke' of the Tyneside workers. By the 1890s the firm was paying Government Duty at an average of £3,000 per week. It was by then the oldest and largest tobacco manufacturer in the North of England and its advertisements often referred to 'the disinfecting qualities of tobacco borne out of the fact that very few tobacco employees were seized during the cholera epidemic or at times of infectious afflictions'.

John Harvey died at Leazes Terrace aged 89, some four years after the death of his much younger business partner and son-in-law, Herbert Davy. Herbert was also American Vice Consul in Newcastle for 33 years.

11. JOHN HAWTHORN, 1808-1866. SURGEON

'Surgeon of this town who died 1866 from Typhus fever taken in the discharge of his duties aged 58. This monument is erected by a few friends and patients of the deceased as a token of respect and esteem.' Typhus was a common illness at this time.

12. ALEXANDER LAING, 1828-1905. WINE MERCHANT AND PATRON OF THE ARTS

In 1900 Newcastle Corporation, aware that Newcastle lacked the sort of art gallery possessed by other important towns and cities, earmarked a site next to the Free Library in New Bridge Street and began to seek subscriptions. When only £1,200 was raised the project seemed doomed. At this point Alexander Laing wrote to the Corporation to announce that 'in commemoration of a successful business career of fifty years in your midst, I am prepared to erect and present to the City a building to be known as the Laing Gallery for the use and enjoyment of the public in perpetuity having no doubt, that by the liberality of the inhabitants it would soon be supplied with pictures and statuary for the encouragement and development of British Art'.

The Laing Art Gallery around 1904.

Born in Forfarshire, Alexander Laing served his time in the drapery trade and worked in Belfast and Edinburgh before arriving in Newcastle in 1849 to represent Jeffrey & Co., the well-known Edinburgh brewers. He later set up on his own account as a bottler then expanded into wines, spirits and the licensed

trade, operating for many years from offices in Market Street.

The Edwardian Baroque Laing Art Gallery, with its Art Nouveau elements was designed by Messrs Cackett and Burns Dick, and was opened in 1904 by Viscount Ridley. In recognition of his generosity in spending over £30,000 for the benefit of his fellow citizens, Alexander Laing was given the Honorary Freedom of the City. The Art Gallery was not built to house an existing collection (Laing had not been a connoisseur or collector). At the opening it did not possess a single work of art and wood shavings were displayed to highlight the gallery's plight.

13. CHRISTOPHER THOMPSON MALING, 1824-1901. POTTERY MANUFACTURER

The Maling family originated in France (as 'de St Malin'), escaped from religious persecution in the 16th century, settled in Filey as merchants and then moved to Sunderland to set up a pottery at North Hylton in 1762.

After over 50 years in Sunderland the pottery was moved to Ouseburn Bridge, Newcastle, where there were better business opportunities. Robert Maling (1781-1863) initiated this move as he manufactured chiefly for the Dutch market and the extensive

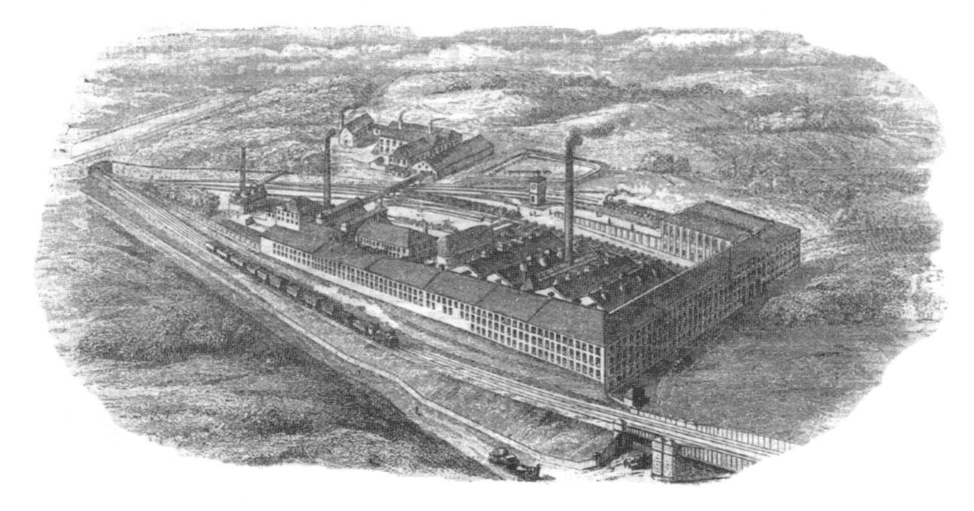

Maling's Ford 'B' factory in the 1880s.

shipping trade of the Tyne must have been an attraction.

Under Christopher Thompson Maling, son of Robert, the business was to reach its peak as the largest pottery in Britain, and possibly the world. In 1857 he married Mary Ford, the daughter of an Edinburgh glassmaker, and with her generous dowry was able to build a new Ouseburn factory two years later, that, with the aid of steam, could produce in one week what had previously taken a year. Production consisted mainly of wholesale commercial pottery, such as the humble earthenware jam jar, and assisted by the custom of Keillers of Dundee, Malings supplied about 95 per cent of the UK market. The factory became known as the Ford Pottery (later Ford A) of Ford Street after Mrs Maling's maiden name – the site today is occupied by a scrap metal business.

In 1878 an even larger self-contained factory, Ford B, was built about half a mile away along Walker Road, which eventually employed about 1000 people, mainly women, who because of the dust became known as 'Maling's White Mice'. Production increased 12-fold.

Ford A closed in 1927 owing to trade depression and overseas competition, while the larger Ford B survived until 1963.

14. JOHN MAWSON, 1815-1867. CHEMIST, VICTIM OF THE TOWN MOOR EXPLOSION

Born near Penrith, John Mawson had been apprenticed to a chemist and druggist in Sunderland, and eventually opened a shop in Mosley Street, Newcastle, aged 28. A few years later he also became sole proprietor of the Northumberland and Newcastle Homeopathic Dispensary in Hood Street, partly on a site that the later well-known business of Mawson Swan and Morgan was to occupy. Two years before his death he took Joseph Wilson Swan (inventor of the electric incandescent lamp and various photographic processes) into partnership to become 'Mawson and Swan'.

When John Mawson became Sheriff in 1867 little did he realise that he would be the first not to complete his year of office because of tragic circumstances occurring a few weeks later.

Nine canisters of nitro glycerine (used in mines for blasting) and equivalent to over four tons of gunpowder had lain for several months uncollected in a cellar at the White Swan Inn Yard, Cloth Market. Understandably, there was some reluctance to go near the dangerous containers. Eventually, a magistrate's warrant was issued for its removal and John Mawson, as a chemist and sheriff, was asked for advice as to the best way of disposing of the substance. His

answer was to use old mine workings on the Town Moor near the relatively new, but temporary, Fever Hospital. A party of seven set out to deal with the problem and the contents (an oily green liquid) of six of the canisters were poured down a shaft. Because the contents of the other three had crystallised and could not be poured away there was a hiatus in the proceedings and the cannisters exploded 'like an earthquake' with 'pieces of flesh and limbs torn from their sockets lying scattered about' and the noise being heard up to 15 miles away. Five of the party died instantly and both John Mawson and Thomas Bryson (Town Surveyor) were blinded, deafened and were to die two days later from their injuries. The wooden hospital, empty at the time, suffered some damage from the blast. John Mawson's funeral procession, nearly two miles long, consisted of around 100 carriages, 2,000 official mourners, and thousands more lining the route. As a mark of respect, businesses in Newcastle and Gateshead were closed and church bells rang muffled peals.

15. JOHN MORRISON, 1792-1858. INVENTOR OF TRANSPARENT ADHESIVE PLASTER

Morrison's sticking plaster, of which he was the only manufacturer, was sold by all chemists in penny packets. A gross could be sent, carriage free, to any address for seven shillings.

16. JOHN INNES NISBET, 1866-1910. MURDERED ON THE ALNMOUTH TRAIN

Murder in English railway carriages was quite sensational when on the morning of 18 March 1910 John Innes Nisbet, aged 44, of Heaton Road, was found dead under a carriage seat with gunshot wounds to the head, at Alnmouth Station, in Northumberland. The weapon was never found.

Nisbet was a clerk/book-keeper employed by the Stobswood Colliery, near Widdrington, and had boarded the train at Newcastle intending to alight at Widdrington to pay the colliery wages. The payout was a regular fortnightly procedure and on this occasion Nisbet's locked black

RAILWAY TRAGEDY.

:o:

Newcastle Clerk Murdered

ROBBERY OF £370 IN GOLD.

Intended as Pitmen's Pay at Stobswood.

MYSTERIOUS CIRCUMSTANCES.

leather bag contained the relatively large sum of £370 9s 6d in gold sovereigns, silver and copper.

Investigation was to establish that the murder had been committed between the stations of Stannington and Morpeth and a reward of £100 was offered for vital information. Three days later John Alexander Dickman, a bookmaker's clerk, with financial difficulties, was arrested and charged amid much speculation concerning both the accused and the victim. Meanwhile Nisbet's funeral attracted 'a vast concourse eager to gratify their morbid taste that the cemetery gates had to be closed long before the arrival of the cortège'.

It was later felt that Dickman had been the victim of a bad press and a biased jury owing to several dubious circumstances surrounding his life, and that perhaps he should have been tried outside the region. Doubtful assumptions had been made during the trial and in the matter of the identification parade, witnesses had been allowed a secret preview of the accused.

The Court of Criminal Appeal, not long established, refused to intervene as did the Home Secretary, and on the day before the execution London and the country were flooded with handbills bearing in large type the following words:

'Must Dickman be hanged tomorrow? No! No! No!
Wire the Home Secretary at once and wash your hands of complicity in the legal crime.'
Nevertherless Dickman faced the executioner within Newcastle Gaol in Carliol Square some five months after the murder, still protesting his innocence.

17. JANE PALMER 1824-1865. WIFE OF CHARLES MARK PALMER

Jane Robson, daughter of a Newcastle draper, became in 1846 first wife of Charles Mark Palmer the local coal owner and shipbuilder. He built the *John Bowes*, a revolutionary iron-built, steam-powered screw collier, a first for Tyneside. Jane performed the naming ceremony in 1852. She died in 1865, aged 41, having given birth to two sons. Charles remarried in 1867 and again in 1877 and produced four more children.

18. JOHN PETER PARLAND, 1807-1871. CAPTAIN OF THE RUSSIAN GUARDS

Parland was a Captain of the Russian Imperial Guards. He lived for several years at Stotes Hall, overlooking Jesmond Dene, and with his aristocratic manners was a personality of the 1860s, often wearing a sealskin coat.

19. GEORGE HARE PHILIPSON, 1801-1876. COACHMAKER

Atkinson and Philipson was a very successful coachbuilding business with its roots going back to 1794. In 1825 John Atkinson's works in High Friar Street had built the first passenger railway coach, to George Stephenson's order, for the Stockton and Darlington Railway. In 1840 Atkinson took his brother-in-law George Hare Philipson into partnership to form Atkinson & Philipson. By this time the concern had moved to much grander premises in Pilgrim Street with land extending to the rear down to Erick Street (the Odeon Cinema stands on most of the site today). The business flourished here until 1919 when the effect of the mass-produced motor car forced it to close.

George Hare Philipson was born near Wark in Northumberland and was the deputy distributor of stamps for Northumberland before he went into carriage manufacture. The business boomed and went on to become the largest firm of its kind in Britain with a thriving export business and a patronage extending from H.R.H. the Prince of Wales down through the titled and landed gentry. At one time the firm was building around 100 different styles of

The Pilgrim Street premises

coach, producing three railway carriages per week for the local railway companies, and advertising the fact that they always carried a stock of at least 500 carriages.

Philipson lived beside the Pilgrim Street premises, was a church warden, a Sunday-school teacher, helped establish the Royal Victoria Asylum for the Blind, and the Northern Counties Institution for the Deaf and Dumb. He was also a governor of the Infirmary and the Dispensary. He shunned local politics but did become a JP a few years before his death. His eldest surviving son, John Philipson, carried on the business, married a daughter of Dr Bruce (whose Academy he had attended) and was considered a pioneer of technical education in Newcastle. He is also buried in the cemetery.

20. William Rea, 1827-1903. Town organist

He 'devoted more than 40 years to cultivating a love of good music among the people of this city'. In 1860 he was appointed Town Organist at a salary of £150 a year, a post he held until 1890, giving weekly organ and piano recitals in the Town Hall. He died in Summerhill Grove.

21. Archibald Reed, 1766-1842. Six times Mayor of Newcastle

By far the largest and most conspicuous monument in the cemetery is the Gothic pile of Kenton stone erected to the design of John Dobson in memory of Archibald Reed. The Reed family can trace their origins back to Bellingham, by the River Rede, where great grandfather Archibald seems to have been a frugal and industrious businessman.

Archibald was probably born in Chipchase Castle in 1766 which his father (Christopher Soulsby Reed) had inherited from his uncle who had been High Sheriff of Northumberland. His mother, Sarah, daughter of Sir Francis Blake of Twizell had brought a fortune of £10,000 upon her marriage in 1757.

After an education at the Grammar School in Newcastle and an apprenticeship as a mercer, Archibald set up as a woollen draper in Sandhill about 1790. He was to become Mayor on six occasions and had the honour of entertaining the Duke of Wellington in the Mansion House and at a ball at the Assembly Rooms. Each Mayor had a fixed annual allowance of £2,000 and because Reed's expenditure was purely on hospitality and charity he was regarded as an ideal Mayor – there were unscrupulous Mayors, however, and the system was scrapped in 1835.

Archibald died in Leazes Terrace and a wall monument was erected to his memory in St Nicholas Cathedral. The tomb in Jesmond cemetery was constructed in 1843 and consists of a two-stage tower with pinnacled diagonal buttresses and an octagonal spire. The slab on the west side marks the entrance to the vault, which also contains the remains of Archibald Joseph Reed, Arthur Reed and Mary Ann Reed. The tomb is a listed building.

Archibald Reed's elaborate Gothic memorial dominates the cemetery.

22. THOMAS MILES RICHARDSON SENIOR, 1784-1848. ARTIST

Regarded as the Father of Fine Arts in Newcastle, Thomas Miles Richardson had the initiative in 1822 to arrange the first Fine Art Exhibition in the North of England in specially built exhibition rooms added on to his home in Brunswick Place, Newcastle. His aim was to display art and encourage the rising middle class to buy and collect pictures. A few years later the Town Corporation employed John Dobson and Richard Grainger to construct Newcastle's first purpose-built art gallery, a classical stone building in Blackett Street – the Northern Academy of Arts. Sadly, the gallery was never a commercial success, probably being too spacious for the amount of local work available, and after Richardson's death other uses were found for the building before its eventual destruction in the 1970s to make way for the Eldon Square shopping complex.

Born in Newcastle and educated at St Andrew's Parish School where his father was Head Master, Thomas went on to spend several unhappy years apprenticed to and then in business as, a cabinet maker. At 22 he took the chance to succeed his father as headmaster and although poorly paid (£30 per annum plus house) he was delighted to leave the world of joinery and with more leisure time available indulge in his talent for landscape and marine painting.

Intending to become a professional painter, Richardson later resigned the headship but then suffered much financial anxiety and with a large family to support was forced back into teaching art in spite of never having received formal training. In later life he regretted not having spent some years in London where experience and contacts might have benefitted him. Some of his better known works include *View of Newcastle from Gateshead Fell* (1816), *A View of the Old Fish Market, Newcastle* (1823), *A View of the Side, Newcastle* (1835).

Richardson's engraving of the Keep, c.1826.

23. JOHN ROACH, 1809-1865. WEST INDIAN, EATING HOUSE PROPRIETOR

Of West Indian origin, John Roach kept an eating house on Grey Street for several years. His widow married J.D. Green, buried next to Roach, continuing the business through the 1870s.

24. WILLIAM SPENCER, 1783-1839. STEEL MANUFACTURER

William's brother, John, began manufacturing steel files in 1810 at Fighting Cocks Yard in the Bigg Market, moving to Newburn in 1822.

25. THOMAS STOKOE, 1812-1877. SAILCLOTH MANUFACTURER

Thomas Stokoe produced sailcloth, canvas and tarpaulins at Lime Street, Lower Ouseburn.

26. JOHN CAMERON SWAN, 1827-1916. MERCHANT

The eldest brother of Sir Joseph Wilson Swan, inventor of the incandescent electric light bulb.

27. 'GENERAL' TERROT, 1758-1839. LIEUTENANT GENERAL CHARLES TERROT, ROYAL ARTILLERY

'He served King and country actively and faithfully for nearly 50 years in Europe, Asia and America, and died in the firm and assured hope of everlasting life … '

28. JOHN HUMBLE TODD, -1881. VALET TO PRINCE JOSEPH NAPOLEON BONAPARTE

A great nephew of Napoleon Bonaparte, Prince Imperial Joseph Napoleon Bonaparte was killed fighting with the British Army against the Zulus in 1879, aged 23 years.

29. JOE WILSON, 1841-1875. SONGWRITER AND RELUCTANT PUBLICAN

Considered by many to have been Newcastle's most successful songwriter, Joe Wilson focussed on working-class life and produced such well-known songs as *Keep Yor Feet Still Geordie Hinny*, and *Geordy Haud the Bairn.*

Born in Stowell Street, the son of a joiner, his 'sweet tenor voice'

Joe Wilson's on New Bridge Street in the 1990s. Today the pub is called The Stout Fiddler

soon earned him a place as a choir boy at All Saints Church. Apprenticed as a printer his first song book was published three years later and in his leisure time he established popular concerts in the working men's clubs which had been newly formed as a counter attraction to the pubs. Turning professional later on, he starred at the Oxford Music Hall in the Cloth market and then toured the North of England as well as selling his home-produced song books at a halfpenny each.

Married in 1869, Joe found travelling and wedded bliss did not mix and two years later became landlord of the Adelaide Hotel on New Bridge Street (later called Joe Wilson's and today The Stout Fiddler). Disillusioned, after a short period he returned to the stage, simultaneously working as a printer to eke out a living. He turned teetotal, and began to write temperance songs that sadly never sold well.

A monument in the form of a broken column (to signify a life cut short) was erected by Thomas Allan, publisher of *Tyneside Songs*, with inscribed lines that Joe used to describe the purpose of his life:

'It's been me aim t'hev a place
I'th' hearts o' the Tyneside people,
Wi' writin' bits o'hyemly sangs
Aw think they'll sing.'

An angel attached to a cross near the gate in the North West cemetery.

An entrance to the catacombs.

This late 19th century damaged headstone to the William Cooper family is in the East Cemetery.

The South West Cemetery

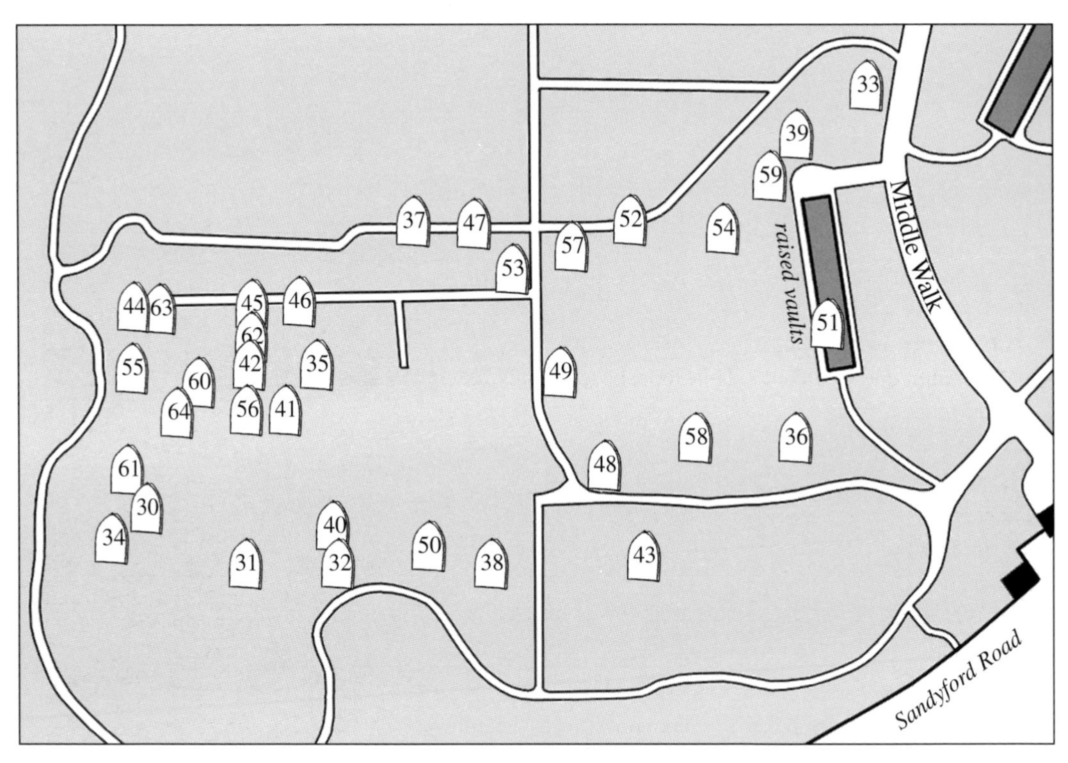

30. Ad Urceolum Foeminas
31. William Armstrong
32. J.S. Arnison
33. Frederick Beavan
34. Ann Black
35. John Blackmore
36. David Burn
37. Hedley Chapman
38. Emerson Charnley
39. Robert Deuchar
40. John Dobson
41. Mark Frater
42. Patrick Freeman
43. Thomas G. Gibson
44. Edward Glynn
45. John & Benjamin Green
46. Sir C.F. Hamond
47. Albany & John Hancock
48. George Y. Heath
49. Charles E. Henzell
50. Thomas Hodgson
51. Thomas W. Keenleyside
52. Benjamin May
53. William Milburn
54. Susan Nesbit
55. Camborne H. Paynter
56. Addison Potter
57. Robert Robinson
58. Robert Robson
59. Walter Runciman
60. Jane Sopwith
61. Aubone Surtees
62. Lewis Thompson
63. Henry West
64. William B. Wilkinson

The South West Cemetery

'Quiet consummation have,
And renowned be thy grave'
Shakespeare, Cymbeline

30. Ad Urceolum Foeminas

This very unusual memorial is not dated and the only inscription is in Latin which reads: 'Ad urceolum foeminas et auriconium valde defletos hunc cippum pater mater que dedicant'. This loosely translates as: 'Father and Mother dedicate this memorial with many tears to Little Pitcher, Little Woman and Golden Hair'. The three children are two boys and a girl. On top of the stone are carved a broken vase and two broken-off rosebuds, to represent the children.

31. William Armstrong, 1817-1884. Master Printer

His monument was 'erected by Mr Joseph Cowen M.P. as a tribute to the virtues of a good and faithful servant of the Newcastle Chronicle for a period of 49 years.'

32. Joseph Simpson Arnison, 1820-1892. Brewer

One-time owner of the nearby Sandyford Brewery

33. Frederick Beavan, 1846-1928. Founder of Beavan's department store

Founder of the once well-known Shields Road department store and grandson of one of Nelson's surgeons at Trafalgar in 1805.

34. Ann Black, 1800-1866. Servant

'Who for nearly 50 years had been the faithful servant and attached Friend in the family of the late William Woods Esq.'

35. JOHN BLACKMORE, 1802-1844. CIVIL ENGINEER

John Blackmore died aged 42 on 15th March 1844, as a result of having scalded himself in a steam bath. He was responsible for the construction of the Newcastle and Carlisle Railway, first as assistant to the engineer, and then as operative engineer. In 1838 the 60-mile line was opened, Blackmore having constructed the first Scotswood railway bridge (destroyed by fire in 1860). He also designed the rail-road bridge at Wylam which was probably the first of its kind in the world. Blackmore, at the height of his engineering career, was living in an elegant house at 3 Greenfield Place, Summerhill, with an office in the Arcade in Newcastle when he met with his unfortunate fatal accident. He left around £5,000 to his widow, Ann née Nixon, and his two young daughters.

36. DAVID BURN, 1797-1873. MERCHANT AND IRONFOUNDER

Ran the Busy Cottage Ironworks with W. Rayne at what is now Pets' Corner, Jesmond Dene.

37. HEDLEY CHAPMAN, JUNIOR 1844-1916. FURNITURE MANUFACTURER

The Chapman story is one of Victorian enterprise and family business, which like many other Victorian ventures, still keeps its name today. Hedley Chapman senior, the son of a harpoon maker, laid the foundations of the future 'Siesta' furniture business when he opened a factory and shop in a busy part of North Shields in 1847. Originating from the Shotley Bridge area it is believed the Chapman family were connected with the sword making and sharpening trade, having been German immigrants in the 16th century.

Hedley Chapman, junior, a child of three when the North Shields shop was opened, was taken into partnership by his enterprising father in 1866 at a time when the factory was producing high quality furniture at its 'steam cabinet works' as well as operating as ships' joiners, brass bedstead makers and undertakers. They were also agents for 'the Metallic Airtight Coffin Company'.

Chapman's shop on Northumberland Street in the 1920s.

In 1871 a branch was opened in Northumberland Street, Newcastle, on a site covered today by Marks & Spencer. Hedley junior managed these Newcastle showrooms while brother William looked after the North Shields workshops where by 1900 about 40 cabinet makers and 40 upholsterers were employed to meet the growing demand for Chapman products.

Further expansion occurred in the 1920s and finally in 1936 'Alfred's' building on the corner of Northumberland Street and Prudhoe Street was acquired to create a desirable 60 metre shop frontage, sold to Marks and Spencer ten years later. The next move was to the corner of Jesmond Road and the Great North Road, complete with private carpark and colourful rock garden. The building of the motorway triggered their final move to Siesta House in Market Street where Chapman's still flourishes.

38. EMERSON CHARNLEY, SENIOR, 1781-1845. BOOKSELLER

Newcastle's medieval bridge accommodated houses and shops along its length and it was to one of these shops that the 14-year-old William Charnley, father of Emerson, came in 1741 to begin a seven-year apprenticeship to a bookseller. William's own career as a bookseller and publisher duly began in 1750 but became unstuck in 1771 when part of the old bridge collapsed in a disastrous flood. Bankruptcy followed but in 1773 a new shop opened at the foot of the Groat Market. William and his wife Elisabeth produced seven children but tragedy dogged them. Three of the children died in infancy while a further three were judged insane. Emerson was the only one fit to succeed to the business on his father's death in 1803. Three years later the construction of Collingwood Street provoked a move further up the Bigg Market and the shop re-opened near the junction with Pudding Chare on the present site of a photographic shop, and there it remained for 66 years.

Emerson, who had received a grammar school education, was described as tall, portly and ungainly. He was often to be seen standing outside his shop, snuff box in hand, ready to engage in conversation with passers-by. But he was a Town Councillor too and his shop became the headquarters of the 'Whig clique' (reformers) who met in a room at the back of the shop – reputedly dark and cluttered.

Well-known throughout Northumberland and Durham as an enthusiastic collector of local literature and undoubtedly acquainted with the engraver Thomas Bewick, he died in his home above the shop aged 63, leaving a son of the same name to carry on the business. Emerson was a prominent member of the Literary and Philosophical Society where a portrait of him hangs today.

39. ROBERT DEUCHAR, 1831-1904. BREWER AND PROPERTY SPECULATOR

Robert, with his three younger brothers, arrived in Newcastle from Forfarshire in the 1860s and from small beginnings as an innkeeper in Newgate Street (the Chancellor's Head) prospered to such an extent that by 1900 he owned 40 licensed houses on Tyneside, a brewery at Duddingston (Edinburgh) employing about 300 people, and the Sandyford Stone Brewery on Sandyford Road.

The Sandyford Stone Brewery probably dates from the mid 18th century and was built of local stone from a quarry alongside Sandyford burn close to Lambert's Leap. It was largely rebuilt around 1840. Several years after buying the brewery in 1892 Robert converted it into a bottling store, offices and a bonded warehouse. A stone door lintel reading 'Office 1904 Robert Deuchar Ltd' can be seen above a Sandyford Road entrance. This photograph was taken around

1965, some 20 years before the building was converted into apartments and offices. For the last ten years of his life he lived at Shortridge Hall close to High Buston, near Warkworth, and after his death the business was continued by his eldest son, Farquhar and descendants, until bought by Newcastle Breweries in 1953.

Robert, no stranger to property speculation, bought South Jesmond House and its grounds (once the home of William Armstrong, father of Lord Armstrong) about 1902. He had the house demolished and the area laid out as building sites for terraced housing. The eventual streets were given names with family connections: Farquhar Street, Shortridge Terrace, Buston Terrace and, of course, Deuchar Street.

40. JOHN DOBSON, 1787-1865. ARCHITECT

Robust, teetotal and an insomniac (only sleeping four or five hours a night) describe some of the personal characteristics of John Dobson, so it is hardly surprising that in a career spanning over 50 years he was involved in a great many projects. He worked mainly in the North but also nationwide building country houses and their grounds for the gentry (which he liked doing best) through to all types of work including domestic, ecclesiastical, industrial, public, railway and port structures. Jesmond Old Cemetery and its buildings were also designed by him. The original memorial to 'JD' lies in front of the 20th century headstone.

Born at the Pineapple Inn, Chirton, North Shields, Dobson was the son of a market gardener and publican and from an early age he demonstrated an artistic talent. His botanical drawings earned him money in his teens when he created designs for a local damask and linen weaver.

For about five years he was apprenticed to Newcastle's and the North East's leading architect, David Stephenson, after which he moved to London to study watercolour, occasionally exhibiting at the Royal Academy, and very nearly becoming a professional artist. However, he returned to Newcastle in 1810 to set up in business as an

John Dobson's Central Station c.1860.

architect and win his first known commission – the design of the Royal Jubilee School in City Road (now demolished). His drawing ability was to give his career an added dimension as he could provide his prospective clients with accurate illustrations as well as architectural plans.

Perhaps his greatest success was the design for Newcastle Central Station, c.1848, which, if the money had been available, would have been the finest railway station outside London. Although the envisaged design never materialised he had the satisfaction of knowing that his innovative curved shed roof of cast iron columns supporting wrought iron ribs with timber and glass in between was the first of its type and became the model for later stations.

He built a house for himself on New Bridge Street which he was to occupy for over 40 years until his death (today it forms part of licensed premises near to the Posthouse Hotel) when he was reckoned to have left a modest estate of £16,000 but a huge legacy of lasting monuments, including Old Eldon Square. One of his children, Alexander was killed in the Great Tyneside Fire of 1854 (see page 52).

41. MARK FRATER, 1805-1861. TAX COLLECTOR AND VICTIM OF A FATAL STABBING

Mark Frater was murdered in broad daylight on 1 October 1861 as he was about to enter his Blackett Street offices. His attacker was George Clark, an unmarried 45-year-old chairmaker who lived at St Nicholas Churchyard in a two-room dwelling. Frater was stabbed in the neck with such force that the table knife used in the attack was bent, and because his windpipe and arteries were instantly severed, he quickly choked to death.

A resident of Bulman's Village near Gosforth, Frater had been a tax collector for several years. Because George Clark had, some months earlier, refused to pay his dog licence fee of six shillings, it became Frater's task to enforce the debt by confiscating property to its value. Clark's response to the order was to sell

all his tools for cash and then find work with an employer who would provide tools for him. However, Clark, who had previous convictions for assault, began to brood over his dilemma. He saw no reason to pay his dog licence fee, and openly encouraged his fellow workers not to do so. He is quoted as saying: 'I will blow their brains out if they come again for the money.' It may have been the escalating debt and the very real threat of having to quit his home that precipitated Clark's lethal and tragic attack on Frater.

Clark was seized at the scene by two witnesses and at the police station readily admitted the crime: 'He robbed me and I robbed him.' Although guilty of murder, Clark was declared insane at his trial and spent the rest of his days in a lunatic asylum.

42. Patrick Freeman II, 1816-1894, Patrick Freeman III, 1845-1888. Millers

The Freeman family were tenant farmers and corn millers in the High Heaton area of Newcastle for several decades before land development forced them away in the 1860s. However, their name is remembered locally in such names as Freeman Hospital, Freeman Road and Paddy Freeman Park – a privilege usually reserved for landowners and politicians. Their farmhouse stood near the main entrance to Paddy Freeman's Park, on a site now occupied by Anscomb Gardens. The corn mill they operated, with a history said to date back at least to the 13th century, is now a ruin and stands close to Lord Armstrong's artificially created waterfall in Jesmond Dene.

The first Patrick Freeman left the Windmill Hills area of Gateshead in the 1790s for High Heaton to farm and mill as a tenant of Sir Matthew White Ridley of Heaton Hall. He died in 1840 and was buried at Westgate Hill Cemetery where his wife had been interred some years before.

Patrick II carried on the business as farmer, working an area of 270 acres with six labourers, and as a miller initially at the Jesmond Dene site, and then after about 1851, two miles downstream at Ouseburn Bridge. A few years later, after Lord Armstrong acquired most of the land on either side of the valley, Patrick left the area for Cambois Farm near Blyth on land also owned by the Ridleys.

Freeman Mill before W.G. Armstrong created the waterfall in Jesmond Dene during the 1860s.

Patrick III died six years before his father and at his death was managing the Look Out Farm at Seaton Delaval, opposite Delaval Hall. The 'broken column' gravestone represents a life cut short.

43. Thomas George Gibson, 1830-1911. Solicitor

Councillor for All Saints, Mayor in 1882, and property owner in the Gibson Street area.

44. Edward Glynn, 1817-1871. Solicitor

He was one of the first promoters of the Shoeblack Brigade, a charity which assisted destitute boys, in Newcastle. He was also instrumental in establishing the first Fire Brigade in Newcastle after the devastation of the great fire and explosions of 1854 (see page 52).

45. John Green, 1787-1852, Benjamin Green, 1811-1858. Architects

John Green was born near Corbridge, the son of a village carpenter. Talented and hard working, he became a successful architect-builder and moved first to Corbridge and then to Newcastle where two of his better known works are the Literary and Philosophical society (1822) and the old Scotswood Suspension Bridge (1831). Green introduced the structural use of laminated tim-

ber, initially for the arches of the Ouseburn and Willington rail viaducts of 1839, which were renewed in iron 30 years later. The painting below, by J.W. Carmichael (c.1841), features the Ouseburn Bridge with the 18th century lead works in the foreground. For several years John was also architect to the estates of the Duke of Northumberland.

Benjamin Green, son of John, was specially trained by Pugin the architect and entered business with his father in the 1830s. Today it is difficult to distinguish between their work but generally John superintended bridge and engineering work while Benjamin planned public buildings, churches and villas. The father's style was plain and economical while Benjamin tended to be elaborate and expensive. Perhaps the best-known buildings in Newcastle credited to them are the Theatre Royal by John and Benjamin (1837) and Grey's Monument by Benjamin (1838). The Greens were extremely busy during the railway building boom with John designing some of the bridges while it is said that 'all the stations between Newcastle and Berwick were built from Benjamin's drawings and were more like the buildings of retired tradesmen than residences for railway officers.'

The Ouseburn Viaduct in 1841.

46. SIR CHARLES FREDERIC HAMOND, 1817-1905. BARRISTER, SHIPOWNER, MP

Responsible for the creation of Leazes Park and the building of Gallowgate baths.

47. ALBANY HANCOCK, 1806-1873, JOHN HANCOCK, 1808-1890. NATURALISTS

At the death of naturalist Albany Hancock, in 1873, his brother John proposed the building of a fine Natural History Museum in his memory because the existing museum, tucked in behind the Literary and Philosophical Society in Westgate Road for nearly 40 years, was proving too cramped and inconvenient.

Six years later a suitable site became available just to the north of Barras Bridge where the property at St James Place was up for sale – Colonel Joicey bought the land, John Hancock set about raising the necessary finance, and John Wardle was engaged as architect. In 1884 the new building, in the classical style, having cost about £500,000 was opened by the Prince and Princess of Wales. John Hancock died a few years later and as a tribute to both brothers the building became the Hancock Museum.

The Hancock Museum, c.1890.

Albany qualified as a solicitor but resigned after only two years in practice, devoting himself to natural history and in particular the study of sealife. Awarded a gold medal by the Royal Society in 1846, he corresponded with leading naturalists including Darwin and Huxley, produced 74 books and papers and was a talented water-colourist.

John Hancock, with his brother Thomas, ran the long-established family hardware shop at Sandhill, but as a keen ornithologist he too found the lure of natural history too strong, and at times of bird-migration, or after a storm, was known to leave home at 3 a.m. to walk to the coast for interesting observations and specimens. An expert taxidermist, he was a contributor at the International Exhibition of 1851 in London.

Albany and John never married and their sister, Mary, who outlived her five brothers and sisters, was for many years John's housekeeper at St Mary's Terrace opposite the Museum.

48. GEORGE YEOMAN HEATH, 1819-1892. SURGEON

Regarded as a fine surgeon who could remove a stone from the bladder in two minutes – a vital asset before the days of anaesthetic.

49. CHARLES EDWARD HENZELL, 1863-1884

… 'who was injured on board the Italian turret ship Giovanni Bausan in 1884 and died in Walker Hospital on the following day aged 21 years.' He had been scalded to death by a burst boiler pipe as the gunboat was being fitted out at the Armstrong Mitchell Yard, Walker.

50. THOMAS HODGSON, 1785-1850. EDITOR OF THE NEWCASTLE CHRONICLE

'Joint proprietor and editor of the Newcastle Chronicle for upwards of 40 years'.

51. THOMAS WILLIAM KEENLEYSIDE, 1798-1867. SOLICITOR

This touching canopied tomb (see over), c.1842, with four slender octagonal piers and tudor arches, was erected as a memorial to the Keenleyside children. They died in a cholera epidemic of 1841-42 – wealth being no protection from infection and a contaminated water supply. Eleanor, the third daughter died 9 December 1841 aged two, followed by Charles the eldest son on 24 December aged 12, and James the second son died 1 January 1842, aged 10.

Tragedy visited the family again in 1870 when a daughter, Louisa Parker, died shortly after giving birth to a grandchild who also died. The Keenleysides lived in Carlton House, Carlton Terrace, now Jesmond Road; the house is still there. Thomas William Keenleyside was a solicitor and alderman. The tomb is a listed structure.

The Keenleyside tomb.

52. BENJAMIN MAY, 1870 -1892. STUDENT

'Student of medicine aged 22 years who was accidentally drowned while rowing on the River Tyne in 1892.'

53. WILLIAM MILBURN, 1826-1903. SHIPPING MAGNATE

Milburn House at Side is a well-known Newcastle building, but the Milburn family commemorated in its name is not so familiar today. Two pubs, a printing works (badly damaged by fire), shops and old housing were demolished to make way for the splendid new office block completed in 1905. Bewick's workshop and Collingwood's birthplace were two notable casualties. Milburn House was built with finance provided by the Milburn family and because of family connections with the world of shipping is designed like a luxury ocean-going liner with floors labelled deck-style with 'A' at the top and working down to 'G' on the ground floor. There are many features of artistic interest such as gesso work and stained glass. Because of the steeply sloping site there are five entrances to the street at four different levels and in the early days about 100 tenants provided employment for nearly 1,000 persons.

William Milburn was born in Ashington in 1826. The son of a ship owner, he married into another ship owning family when he wed Mary Davison of Blyth. Milburn possessed some of the finest and fastest sailing ships of the day – one vessel holding the record of 68 days for the run to New Zealand. Later he was one of the first to adopt steam in the freight trade. The business of Wm. Milburn & Co. became international, including the China tea trade, and at one time was ranked among the top five in the

A busy Newcastle Quayside in the 1880s.

world tonnage league. Eventually it was to be coal from Ashington Colliery, the largest and one of the most prosperous collieries in Britain, and its export from the port of Blyth that was to give even greater impetus to his business.

William Milburn's son, John Davison Milburn (1851-1907) was born at Blyth, educated at Dr Bruce's Academy in Newcastle and at Brampton, before becoming a partner in the business. He later became a director/chairman of several North East companies, a JP for Northumberland, and the High Sheriff for the county in 1905, in which year he was created a baronet.

54. SUSAN NESBIT, 1789-1862. SERVANT

'For 60 years a faithful and highly valued servant in the family of Ralph Park Philipson, solicitor.' She is buried with the Philipson family, for whom she had begun work at the age of 13.

55. CAMBORNE HASTINGS PAYNTER, 1836-1854. VICTIM OF THE FIRE OF 1854

Camborne Hastings Paynter's gravestone reads: 'Ensign in the 26th Cameronians. This promising young officer was killed on 6th October 1854 by the terrific explosion at Gateshead while engaged with a party of his Regiment in endeavouring to arrest the progress of the conflagration.' The young soldier was 18 years old. He was fighting the flames on the Gateshead side of the Tyne when tons of burning rubbish in Hillgate collapsed, burying him and several others, including Alexander Dobson, the son of John Dobson, architect.

The great fire of 1854, which devastated both sides of the Tyne, left many dead and the damage cost between £300,000 and £400,000. The flames could be seen 50 miles away.

56. Addison Potter, 1820-1894. Owner of Heaton Hall

A businessman, and Mayor in 1873 and 1874, Potter sold part of Heaton Hall estate to Newcastle Corporation in 1879. It became Heaton Park. The Hall was demolished in the 1930s.

57. Robert Robinson, 1817-1903. Bookseller

Robinson's bookshop started off in 1840 at the corner of Shakespeare Street. The premises were known as the 'Bewick's Head'. There may be a family connection with Robinson's booksellers in the Grainger Market and the Robinson Library of Newcastle University. Robinson published Thomas Bewick's 'His Life and Times' and often slept among his treasured books.

58. Robert Robson 1812-1878. Furniture manufacturer

For about a century Robson's furniture and furnishings store stood on Northumberland Street, at its corner with Saville row, gradually expanding in size as its quality products grew in reputation.

Robert Robson, upholsterer and cabinet maker, established the business in 1835 in a small house on the opposite side of Northumberland Street (at the corner of Elswick Court, now engulfed by Fenwick's Department Store) where he lived and worked for nearly 30 years. He had served his apprenticeship as a cabinet maker on Pilgrim Street. His father, Edward had been a forester on the Bowes Lyon estate at Gibside

Robson's, right, faces Fenwick's proudly across Northumberland Street at the turn of the century. The business had been first established in the little shop just beyond Fenwick's.

(Co. Durham) and at Glamis Castle on Tayside before returning to Newcastle to manage a seed merchant's shop in the Haymarket.

Two of Robson's sons followed their father in the flourishing furniture business. Another son, Frederick, founded the well-known optician's business on Pilgrim Street, F. Robson & Co. In addition to retail sales much work took place at hotels, churches, public buildings and on board several of the ocean liners being built on the Tyne – in particular *Mauretania*. Later on contracts were taken at some of the region's stately homes, notably Alnwick Castle, Wallington and Cragside.

Some two years after Robert's death, a cabinet factory was built at Spital Tongues where over 200 were employed, houses built for employees, and streets named after some of the great furniture pioneers (Sheraton, Chippendale). Huge stocks of timber were seasoned and dried here for periods of up to three years in order to produce the dry wood Robson considered essential for good furniture. The factory also had its own private fire brigade.

The business passed through the hands of four generations before it was finally taken over by the Maple Group in 1953.

59. WALTER RUNCIMAN, 1847-1937. SHIPOWNER, PHILANTHROPIST AND MP

He founded the Moor shipping line and lived in Fernwood House, Jesmond. Created a baronet in 1906, his column, almost lost in trees and brambles, is one of the tallest in the cemetery.

60. JANE SOPWITH, 1807-1855. WIFE OF THOMAS SOPWITH, CIVIL ENGINEER

Jane Scott married Thomas Sopwith in 1831, giving birth to nine children, two of them buried here, before her death. Jane was Thomas's second wife – his first, Mary, had died in childbirth after less than a year of marriage. Thomas's third wife was Anne Potter of Heaton Hall.

61. AUBONE SURTEES, 1777-1859. WINE AND SPIRITS IMPORTER AND COALOWNER

Aubone Surtees, Mayor in 1821, was the nephew of Bessie Surtees who eloped with John Scott.

62. LEWIS THOMPSON, 1812-1889. BENEFACTOR OF BYKER

Lewis Thompson left the handsome sum of £15,000 to the township of Byker in 1889 the interest on which was to reduce the poor rate for ever, provided that the

guardians of Byker kept the family tomb in good repair and placed a memorial garland valued at not less than two shillings on the tomb annually. Failure to comply with either of these conditions for a period of three successive years meant the £15,000 would revert to the British nation – which presumably it now has. Lewis Thompson himself was a chemist specialising in coal gas and gas lighting.

63. HENRY WEST, 1786-1861. CAPTAIN, RN

A veteran of the Battle of Trafalgar, he lived at 1 Jesmond Gardens.

64. WILLIAM BOUTLAND WILKINSON, 1819-1902. INVENTOR OF REINFORCED CONCRETE

WILKINSON'S
CEMENT CONCRETE FLOORING,

William Boutland Wilkinson was probably so busy with his plastering contracts and the laying of concrete floors that he neglected to take out a patent for the invention of reinforced concrete, and though William was aware of the technique as early as 1854, it was a Frenchman, Joseph Monier, who received the credit in 1867.

William, one of three children, was born at St Peter's, Tyneside, the son of a potter. He was educated at Bruce's Academy in Percy Street. Apprenticed to a plasterer, he later set up business in New Bridge Street as a 'Plaster of Paris and Roman Cement Manufacturer'. In 1865 he built what may have been the first reinforced concrete building in the world behind his home in Ellison Place as a small cottage for his foreman. It was demolished in 1954 to make way for Newcastle Polytechnic. He held several directorships including 26 years on the board of Newcastle and Gateshead Water Co. During his life he gave generously to the Church of England and in St Nicholas cathedral (north ambulatory) a stained glass window by Kempe is dedicated to his memory.

William Crawford's iron headstone is now unreadable.
These crowded graves were moved together and reinterred in 1971 from another part of the cemetery.

Dwarfed by a gnarled tree, this urn on a pillar commemorates John Crosier (died 1895) and family.

THE EAST CEMETERY

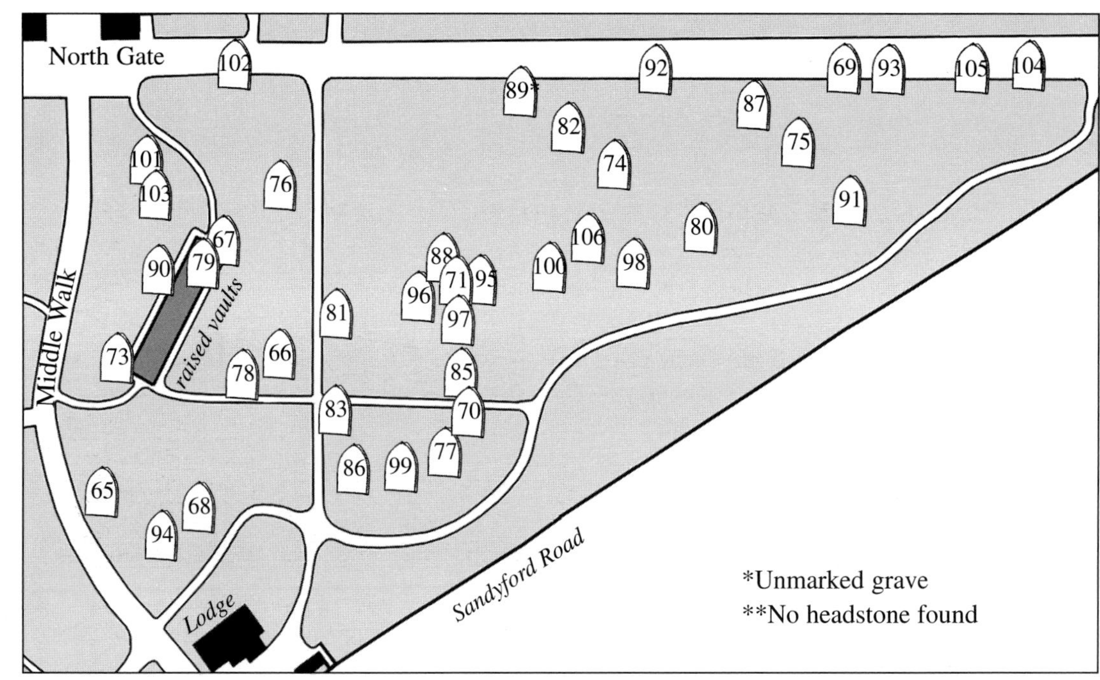

65. William Edwin Adams
66. Luke Armstrong
67. William Armstrong
68. John Arthur
69. E.M. Bainbridge
70. Henry Bowman Brady
71. Charles Bragg
72. Archibald Brown**
73. J.C. Bruce
74. Thomas Bryson
75. Thomas Burt
76. James Coxon
77. William Crawford
78. Thomas Crossling
79. Armorer Donkin
80. Thomas Dunn
81. Joseph Baxter Ellis
82. Elvira
83. John James Fenwick
84. Elizabeth Greenhow**
85. David Haggie
86. Robert Heads
87. John Hewitson
88. John Henry Holmes
89. Margaret Redford Hoy*
90. Benjamin Carr Lawton
91. Henry Murton
92. William Newton
93. Thomas Oliver
94. Carlo Pallotti
95. Jonathan Priestman
96. Joseph Procter
97. Thomas Pumphrey
98. Andrew Reid
99. John Philip Robson
100. Arthur M. Sutherland
101. Frances Swan
102. William Toward
103. Frederick Turnbull
104. Thomas Hall Tweedy
105. John Watson
106. Robert Spence Watson

The East Cemetery

'Golden Lads and Girls all must
Like chimney sweepers come to dust.'
Shakespeare, Cymbeline

65. William Edwin Adams, 1832-1906. Founder of the Dicky Bird Society

Editor of the *Newcastle Weekly Chronicle* and founder of Uncle Toby's Dicky Bird Society, William Edwin Adams was a self-taught and radical man. Originally from Cheltenham and apprenticed to a printer at 14, he energetically undertook his own education and became involved in the Republican movement of the 1850s. He worked for various radical newspapers in Manchester and London before coming to Newcastle in 1863 to work for the *Newcastle Chronicle*. He soon became involved with many aspects of 'progress, culture and humanity' including the establishment of the Free Library and distribution of toys to poor children. The Dicky Bird Society was a column for children, who knew W.E. Adams as 'Uncle Toby' and was all about birds and animals. It was immensely popular and the Dicky Bird Society enrolled thousands of young members who pledged themselves to be kind to all living things. W.E. Adams died and is buried in Madeira but his Newcastle memorial reads: 'Each kindness shown to birds and man/ Is sure to flutter back again'. His bust was presented to the Free Library and it is still held in City Library.

66. Luke Armstrong, 1834-1888. Surgeon at Newcastle Infirmary

He succeeded Dr Gibb (of Blaydon Races fame) as surgeon at the old Infirmary at the Forth, near the Central Station. A scholarship was founded in his memory at the College of Medicine.

67. William Armstrong, 1778-1857. Father of Lord Armstrong

The son of a Cumbrian shoemaker, William came to Newcastle at around 20 years of age to work as a clerk for corn merchants on the Quayside, eventually becoming proprietor. Marrying soon after his arrival in Newcastle, his first home was at 9 Pleasant Row in Shieldfield, a three-storey terrace house with a garden reaching down to Pandon Dene. William George Armstrong was born here in 1810. The house disappeared long ago but the lintel inscribed 'Armstrong House' and a commemoration stone can be seen in the wall opposite Christ Church, Shieldfield. William moved to South Jesmond in 1840. Later in life he entered local politics and as a councillor for the new ward of Jesmond, took a serious interest in the modernisation of the Tyne. He rose to become Alderman and then Mayor. Always a keen mathematician, his collection of nearly 1,300 books were given on his death to the Literary and Philosophical Society, of which he had been a member for nearly 60 years. He was also a founder member of the Natural History Society.

9, Pleasant Row before demolition.

68. JOHN ARTHUR, 1819-1893. COOPER

He founded Arthur's Cooperage on the Quayside adjoining the Long Stairs.

69. EMERSON MUSCHAMP BAINBRIDGE 1817-1892. SHOPKEEPER SUPREME

Emerson Muschamp Bainbridge, founder of Bainbridge's department store, was youngest of seven children born to Cuthbert Bainbridge and Mary Muschamp (whose family had married into the Emersons at an earlier date). Born at Eastgate, Weardale, where his father was a yeoman farmer, he was apprenticed at 13 to a Newcastle draper for five years. During the seven days annual holiday young Emerson usually walked the 30 miles back home – an energy that characterised his life.

After two year's London experience following the end of his apprenticeship, Emerson returned to Newcastle to partner a woollen and linen

Bainbridge & Co., Market Street at the turn of the century.

draper in the new and fashionable Market Street where they were among the very first traders to adopt fixed price labelling rather than the customary haggling. Later innovations included the sale of ready-made clothes and in 1849 departmentalisation – probably the first shop to introduce this. In 1855 Emerson became sole proprietor and from then on his Market Street premises expanded until in 1952 the business was taken over by the John Lewis Partnership, though the name 'Bainbridge' remains. The premises are now in Eldon Square.

The family were staunch Methodists and always tried to deal fairly with both customer and employee. At a time when it was usual to work a 15-hour day, six days a week, with no half-day closing, Emerson allowed time off to staff as follows: 'one evening a week for courting purposes and two if they go to prayer meetings regularly'.

70. HENRY BOWMAN BRADY, 1835-1891. CHEMIST

Founder of Brady & Martin, a well-known firm of chemists, and surgical instrument makers.

71. CHARLES BRAGG, 1801-1874. SHOPKEEPER

He ran a family business of dressmakers, milliners and cabinet makers on Pilgrim Street. He employed John James Fenwick before he left to start his own successful business.

72. ARCHIBALD BROWN, 1830-1905. EMPLOYEE OF COXON'S

His working life for one employer was extremely long. 'For 55 years with James Coxon & Co. of this City. This memorial is erected as a mark of esteem by his fellow colleagues.'

73. JOHN COLLINGWOOD BRUCE 1805-1892. HISTORIAN AND EDUCATIONALIST

The eldest son of a schoolmaster, John Collingwood Bruce, headmaster and historian, was born in Newcastle one year before his father founded the Percy Street Academy which on this 1844 illustration is the large house on the left. A plaque above the present shop frontage at the corner of Percy Street and

St Thomas' Street marks the site of the school.

A basic education with his father was followed by two years in London before John moved on to Glasgow to study medicine. In addition to a medical qualification he also read divinity, obtained a licence to preach, and was set to be a medical missionary when his father's ill health prompted him to return to Newcastle to assist with the teaching at the popular school. In 1834 he assumed the headship upon his father's death and abandoned any idea of becoming a missionary. Boys that he must have known at the Academy included Robert Stephenson, civil engineer and designer of the High Level Bridge and Charles Mark Palmer the shipbuilder, who later achieved international fame.

After 26 years as headmaster John 'transferred the school to other hands' and at the age of 55, devoted the rest of his long life to the study of the Romans in the north. His historical and descriptive account of the Roman Wall is still a work of reference. He became involved in all things educational, charitable and religious, even reviving public interest in Northumbrian folk music. There is a marble effigy of him in St Nicholas' Cathedral.

The photograph of the gravestone of John Collingwood Bruce and his wife, Charlotte, shows us an example of the tragedy that so many families experienced in those days. Their daughter, Frances, died aged 19 months in 1839.

74. THOMAS BRYSON, 1805-1867. TOWN SURVEYOR

Died along with John Mawson and others in the Town Moor explosion of 1867 (see page 26).

75. THOMAS BURT, MP, 1837-1922. PITMAN AND MEMBER OF PARLIAMENT

From pitboy to Privy Councillor neatly summarises the life of Thomas Burt, and he was also the first working miner to become an MP when in 1874 he won the seat for Morpeth as a Liberal (the Labour Party was not yet formed) and continued to hold it until retirement in 1918, by which time he had become 'father' of the House of Commons.

Born near Backworth, Northumberland, Thomas had a limited education at a local dame school before beginning work at ten years old as a pit trapper boy (opening and closing ventilation doors) in darkness where he earned ten pence for a 12-hour day. Both father and son were Primitive Methodists and strictly teetotal.

Thomas became addicted to reading and was frequently to be seen walking to and from Newcastle (18 miles return) to buy second-hand books. He became proficient in Latin, French, mathematics, English literature and shorthand in spite of the crowded conditions of a one-roomed cottage. He married his cousin Mary Weatherburn and is later reported to have said it was: 'the best day's work I have done!' They were together for over 50 years.

In 1895 a new permanent headquarters for the Northumberland Miners' Association was opened at Northumberland Road, Newcastle, later to be named Burt Hall in recognition of Thomas's 48 years as general secretary and three years as Secretary of the Board of Trade. A sculpture of Ralph Hedley's painting of a pitman crowns the roof of the building.

76. JAMES COXON, 1804-1867. FOUNDER OF COXON'S DEPARTMENT STORE

Coxon's was a household name throughout the North of England over three generations as one of the largest drapery stores in Newcastle. The photograph on the following page was taken in the 1920s just before financial difficulties during the depression forced the shop to close in 1928, costing 400 people their jobs. Coxon's stood at the corner of Grey Street and Market Street and the photograph clearly shows the dormitories built on top of the original Grainger building of the late 1830s to house staff from as far afield as Hartlepool and Barnard Castle. The cellar was the domain of the official ferret keeper employed to combat rats from the Turks Head Hotel, round the corner on Grey Street.

Coxon's in the 1920s not long before the purchase of a magnificent Italian marble staircase is said to have contributed to the business's decline.

The business was established in 1830 by James Coxon, from Glanton, Northumberland, who with a Thomas Richardson as partner, ran a drapery and haberdashers' shop in Mosley Street until the move to Market Street in the 1840s. James died at Benton House in 1867 after living for many years in Burdon Place in Brandling Village, and was succeeded by his son Herbert. Herbert's son, another Herbert, carried on the business until 1928.

There were many proposals for the Coxon site including 'the creation of a super cinema' but it was the Sunderland based Binns Ltd that moved in with a view to establishing themselves in Newcastle for the North East Coast Exhibition of 1929. It is said that next-door-neighbours, Bainbridge's, had considered Coxon's selling price too expensive.

77. WILLIAM CRAWFORD, 1787-1844. IRON FOUNDER AT WALKER IRON WORKS

Crawford's memorial (right) is the only iron plate memorial in the cemetery. It is unreadable now but there is a nearby headstone to the same family which may have replaced it.

78. THOMAS CROSSLING, 1829-1888. PLUMBER

Founder of the local firm of plumbers and paint merchants in 1855 on Clayton Street.

79. ARMORER DONKIN, 1779-1851. SOLICITOR

Neighbour and friend of William Armstrong. The young W.G. Armstrong was articled to him as a solicitor.

80. THOMAS DUNN, 1796-1855. ROMAN CATHOLIC MAYOR OF NEWCASTLE

First Roman Catholic Mayor of Newcastle in 1842. The Dunn family gave huge sums of money to St Mary's Roman Catholic Cathedral.

81. JOSEPH BAXTER ELLIS, 1842-1918. KNIGHTED IN 1906

Ran the flour business of Joseph Hindhaugh. Became first Lord Mayor of Newcastle, 1905.

82. ELVIRA, 1861-1913

This simple cross just reveals the Christian name of the woman buried here. The only clue is a legend that a maid named Elvira was murdered at Millfield House in Jesmond Dene. Her ghost supposedly haunts one of the upper windows there. A newspaper death announcement records that an Elvira Youll died at the RVI on 14th February 1913, aged 52, and this must be the Elvira buried here. She had worked for many years for Alderman Anderson of Burdon Terrace. Whether she was the Elvira of the Jesmond Dene legend is not known.

83. JOHN JAMES FENWICK, 1846-1905. OWNER OF FENWICK'S DEPARTMENT STORE

Born at Richmond in Yorkshire and one of 11 children, this son of a grocer attended local schools before moving to Stockton at 14 to become an apprentice draper. Aged 22 he was advised to move to Newcastle for better opportunities and eventually found work at Charles Bragg & Co. of Pilgrim Street, a firm of exclusive silk mercers. Here he quickly rose to become manager at an annual income of £600, but, ambitious as ever, began a sideline business of selling insurance for which he was eventually dismissed. Fenwick took the case to court and was awarded damages of £1,000 for wrongful dismissal – a sum which was to prove useful in opening his first shop at 5 Northumberland Street in 1882 as a 'mantle maker and furrier'. Northumberland Street was at that time a largely residential street dominated by professional men. Ideally the shop was close to the Brunswick Methodist Chapel which was to later play a significant part in John Fenwick's restricted leisure time.

In 1885 two doctors' houses became vacant at 37/39 Northumberland Street and Fenwick quickly moved in to expand his business. The photograph on the following page shows the premises a few years later. Today the site has expanded and become much more

Fenwick's c.1890. Over 100 years later the department store is still on Northumberland Street.

magnificent. With several branches nationwide this family firm employs about 2,500 staff.

Fenwick visited customers in their homes to promote the sale of fashionable clothes. The shop became departmentalised yet kept single article window dressing. He insisted that customers be allowed to browse without being spoken to by assistants.

In 1891 Fenwick opened an exclusive shop in London (New Bond Street) and the venture was assisted a few years later by the publicity gained from the stage production of George Du Maurier's *Trilby*. In recognition of the heroine, Dorothea Baird (later Mrs Henry Irving), having been born on the site of the Newcastle shop, Fenwick made her gown, costume and soft felt hat complete with narrow brim and indented crown. The birth of the trilby hat was complete!

84. ELIZABETH GREENHOW, 1795-1850. WIFE OF THOMAS GREENHOW, SURGEON

In 1820 Thomas Michael Greenhow married Elizabeth, eldest sister of Harriet Martineau the authoress. Thomas was a highly thought of surgeon with an excellent reputation as a 'bold and skilful operator' particularly regarding diseases of the eye. Elizabeth had to withstand some domestic intrusion as the chronically ill Harriet moved into their home at Eldon Square for several months, and then lived nearby at Tynemouth for five years. Elizabeth died in 1850 leaving at least one son while Harriet lived for another 26 years. Thomas remarried and moved to Leeds where he lived to be 90. Elizabeth's headstone cannot be located and may have been lost during the 1971 exhumations.

85. DAVID HAGGIE, 1819-1895. HAGGIE'S ROPEWORKS, GATESHEAD

One of three rope-maker brothers, he was Mayor of Gateshead in 1854, and narrowly escaped death from a falling coping stone in the great fire of that year (see page 52).

86. ROBERT HEADS, 1824-1869. HIGH LEVEL BRIDGE ACCIDENT VICTIM

… 'lost his life on the High Level Bridge by the upsetting of a railway carriage in which he was travelling, the 2nd of August 1869, aged 45 years.' It hardly bears thinking about the suffering of his wife, Eleanor, who, as so often in Victorian times, also had to endure the deaths of three young children – Joseph in 1853 aged five, William in 1853 aged 18 months, Isabella Jane in 1864 aged six.

87. JOHN HEWITSON, 1839-1907. SLATE MERCHANT OF LEAZES PARK ROAD

88. JOHN HENRY HOLMES, 1857-1935. ELECTRICAL ENGINEER

John Henry Holmes founded an electrical engineering business in Portland Road, Shieldfield, in 1883. It was to make a valuable contribution to the development of electric lighting. In the summer of that year Holmes installed electric lighting at 'Wellburn', his father's house at Jesmond, the first private house in Newcastle to be electrically lit. There quickly followed many orders for lighting sets and he developed the now familiar quick break switch with snap-off action, a device which he patented in 1884. The 'Castle' dynamo, one of the earliest to be made in the UK, was developed in the following year and together with train lighting and electrical machinery for many industrial uses the firm's world-wide order book was always full – they even exported portable lighting sets for night navigation on the Suez Canal.

In 1928 the company became part of Reyrolle and Co. Ltd at Hebburn. Only in 1997 were the buildings at Portland Road demolished. A reconstruction of Holmes's workshop with original tools, early lamps and a 'Castle' dynamo is on display at Newcastle Discovery Museum.

John Henry Holmes's father, William Henry, a Quaker, started off in 1845 as a glass manufacturer in South Shields before moving to Newcastle in 1848. He went into paint manufacture and in 1878 built a paint factory on Portland Road, Shieldfield. The plant closed in 1980.

Holmes Electrical Engineering works in Shieldfield c.1890, to the left, with the paint factory on the right.

89. MARGARET REDFORD HOY, 1822-1836. GROCER'S DAUGHTER

The earliest burial in the cemetery, Margaret was buried, aged 14, on 9th December 1836 in an unmarked grave.

90. BENJAMIN CARR LAWTON, 1815-1889. ENGINEER, PUBLIC WORKS CONTRACTOR

Benjamin Lawton, originally from Dewsbury, was an engineer involved with the construction of the Newcastle and Berwick Railway, the railways at Alston and Team Valley, and various bridges. He was also contractor for the masonry work of the High Level Bridge, and the breakwaters for the piers at the mouth of the Tyne. His grave reveals a not untypical story of tragic death and bereavement. His wife, Jane, died in October 1848 aged 36; a son, Thomas, died in January 1849 aged 4; a second wife, Elizabeth, died in July 1850 aged 20; and ten years later a daughter, Sarah Jane, died aged just 17. His last home was in Fern Avenue, Jesmond, and his third wife survived him.

91. HENRY MURTON, 1818-1874. FOUNDER OF MURTON'S STORE.

In 1848 Henry Murton founded an agency for the sale of industrial rubber products next door to the premises of George Angus in Grey Street. His son, Henry Angus Murton continued the business and took over the Angus premises in 1868. In 1902 Henry Angus moved to a Grainger

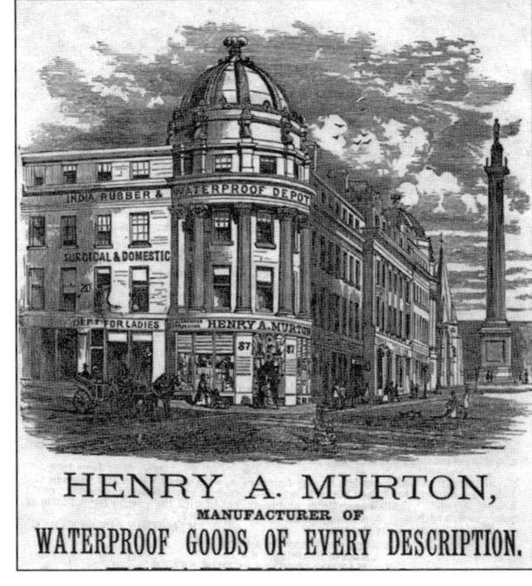

Many will remember Murton's shop at the corner of Grainger Street and the Bigg Market, pictured above in the 1920s. Murton's previously occupied a site on the corner of Market Street and Grey Street.

Street site at the corner of Bigg Market and stayed there as a retail store (sports outfitters, outdoor clothing and accessories) until the shop was sold to the Co-op in 1957. The magnificent tomb, two metres high, with classical pilasters, commemorates many members of the Murton family.

92. Dr William Newton, 1817-1863. Surgeon and social reformer

The son of a Newcastle nurseryman with gardens near Barras Bridge, William Newton completed his education at Edinburgh University where he excelled in both medicine and the classics to return home with five silver medals. By the age of 25 he was in practice as a surgeon and four years later became surgeon to a division of All Saints Parish. He was said to have been at his post night and day in 1853 during the cholera outbreak of that year and to have worked 'like a brick' to prevent further deaths. He was awarded 'a service of silver plate' suitably inscribed and presented to him at a public dinner at the London Tavern in Gibson Street.

In 1851 Newton became a councillor for All Saints East where education and sanitation were high on his agenda, and as an independent he promoted cheap schools, a free library, recreation grounds, baths, wash houses, efficient sewerage and unpolluted water. Eventually he became Chairman of the Schools and Charities Committee. He died tragically young at 46 from injuries sustained in a riding accident on the Town Moor, leaving a widow and three children.

Dog Bank, All Saints, c.1884. Conditions here had not changed very much since Dr Newton fought an outbreak of cholera in 1853.

The eldest son, Henry William (1843-1914) followed his father's career but went on to become Sheriff, Mayor (twice) and a Knight. His tombstone (statue of Christ on a pedestal) is also in the cemetery and records Henry William as being 'Founder of the Public Libraries, 48 years a City Councillor, Honorary Freeman of the City'. Newton Road in High Heaton is named after him.

93. THOMAS OLIVER, 1791-1857. ARCHITECT AND SURVEYOR

As one of a group of architects involved in the transformation of Newcastle into 'Tyneside Classical', Thomas Oliver played a significant role and, of his buildings remaining today, Leazes Terrace and Leazes Crescent are the best-known examples. For his work in surveying the first railway line from Manchester to Liverpool he was offered a knighthood, which he refused (George and Robert Stephenson also declined a title).

Born near Jedburgh, the only son of a weaver who died when Thomas was only two, much of his early life is unknown. He appears to have served an apprenticeship as a mason, with his future father-in-law, probably came to Newcastle at the age of 22, and began working for John Dobson, during which time he married and set up home in High Friar Street.

When he was 30, Oliver set up in business on his own, eventually with an office in the Royal Arcade and a home in Picton Place, where he was to die. Besides his architectural work,

The elegant development of Leazes Terrace as engraved by Collard and Ross in the 1840s.

Oliver surveyed and resurveyed Newcastle to such an extent that he produced various accurate and superbly engraved maps of the town, plus accompanying books, invaluable for local historians. Also a talented artist, he 'drew on the spot' a panoramic view of Newcastle and Gateshead from Windmill Hills for inclusion in his 1830 plan of Newcastle and Gateshead.

One of his seven children, another Thomas (1824-1902) founded the well-known firm of architects Oliver, Leeson and Wood and is also buried in this cemetery.

94. CARLO PALLOTTI, 1855-1890. ITALIAN VICE-CONSUL AND DOCTOR

This elaborately carved Italian marble angel (see also page 4) is now detached from its base and stands in front of the pedestal, which bears an inscription in Italian written by Pallotti's father. At today's prices this angel would cost approximately £7,000. Pallotti lived in Eldon Place.

95. JONATHAN PRIESTMAN, 1787-1863. TANNER AND QUAKER

He owned a tannery at Blackfriars and, with his wife, Rachel Bragg, was a minister in the Society of Friends. They were among the first teetotallers in Newcastle.

96. JOSEPH PROCTER, 1800-1875. FLOUR MILLER, LATER OF LOWER OUSEBURN

Joseph was a miller, working the first steam mill in the North at Willington on Tyne.

97. THOMAS PUMPHREY, 1833-1911. TEETOTALLER AND COFFEE DEALER

Thomas Pumphrey, a Quaker and strict teetotaller, was so appalled at the amount of heavy drinking taking place near his grocer's shop in the Cloth Market area of Newcastle that in 1887 he recognised a business opportunity and converted the first floor of his premises into a café and meeting place. Here he served 'freshly roasted coffee', made from coffee beans actually roasted in small cylinders on the premises, as an alternative to alcohol, and in so doing, is thought to have begun a national trend.

Born in Worcester, the son of a Quaker boarding school superintendent, Thomas first became associated with the grocery business when, at 22, he joined his uncle Henry Richardson in Newcastle. Three years later he became sole proprietor of the shop which had originated in 1750 on the same site. The Cloth Market was then known as the Flesh Market and was part of a much larger market in the old town centre. The premises were rebuilt in 1870 and 40 years later an amalgamation with T. Carrick Watson of Blackett Street formed Pumphrey and Carrick Watson Ltd. Ironically the shop and café have now been replaced by a pub but it is nice to see that Pumphrey's name has been kept together with the words 'Coffee Roaster' and 'Coffee Dealer' below each window.

Thomas married Emma Richardson of Summerhill (from the leather manufacturing family) and thus became related through marriage to John Wigham Richardson (shipbuilder), Robert Spence Watson (solicitor) and John Theodore Merz (scholar and scientist).

98. ANDREW REID, 1823-1896. PRINTER

Andrew Reid was born into a successful Newcastle business family. His Scottish grandfather had founded Reid's the Jewellers, an uncle established the Leazes Brewery, while another owned the Pelton Collieries. Not surprisingly Andrew was to inherit some of this enterprising ability and create what was to become the region's largest printing business. A seven year apprenticeship was served as 'an Engraver and Copper Plate Printer' with Mark Lambert, a former pupil of Thomas Bewick and after 18 months in London gaining valuable experience in the new field of lithographic printing (which could produce maps, plans and paintings more economically) Andrew set up business in a rented room at the corner of Pilgrim Street and Shakespeare Street. He was 22 and called himself 'engraver on silver and copper' but soon turned his attention to general printing, bookbinding and lithography.

Reid's printing works at Side, 1863.

Realising the potential of the new railway system, Andrew rapidly spotted a gap in the market and after about two years in business produced the first of his many publications, *Reid's Railway Rides*, which consisted of a folding map of the London to Edinburgh journey, marking towns, roads, giving mileages and naming stations with refreshment facilities. It

sold well and soon other routes were catered for. Two years later, in 1849, he published the first local railway guide in Britain which was effectively a monthly timetable, together with fares for all classes of passengers, priced at just one penny. Its older rival, Bradshaw, though more comprehensive, sold for a shilling.

Andrew Reid was no longer a mere jobbing printer, often struggling to pay his employees' wages, but about to head a large scale business. Now he served the expanding railway market and was engaged in on major contracts for local colliery owners, the River Tyne Commissioners and Newcastle Corporation. More space for machinery became a priority and in 1863 purpose-built premises were opened at the foot of Akenside Hill, to be known as 'Printing Court Buildings'. Some 50 years later another large development was completed next door, to be known as Akenside House. Printing Court Buildings was demolished to make way for the new Tyne Bridge in 1925 and replacement premises were opened at Strawberry House, Leazes Park Road. Akenside House escaped destruction and today is the pub Akenside Traders.

In 1963 Andrew Reid & Co. Ltd was absorbed by Hindson Print, now Elanders Hindson. Andrew Reid married Ellen Boosey of the celebrated London music printing family and was survived by seven of his 11 children. His widow died in 1925 at the ripe old age of 92. David Reid, also buried nearby in the cemetery, Andrew's father and a goldsmith was the brother-in-law of Michael Faraday, the well-known physicist and chemist.

99. JOHN PHILIP ROBSON, 1808-1890. 'BARD OF THE TYNE AND MINSTREL OF THE WEAR'

John Philip Robson was born in Bailiffgate, beside the Keep in Newcastle. He was orphaned at eight, an errand boy at 11 and then an apprentice plane-maker at Atkinson's coachworks. After an accident prevented him continuing in this work he turned to teaching and literature. Queen Victoria sent him £20 'as a slight recognition of his talents as a poet'. He was a frequent contributor to the local press and at one time a household name in Newcastle. The lines on his stone are now worn away, but once read:

> *'Tho' dead, in lamenting thee, still be it mine*
> *To honour thy name, sweetest bard of the Tyne.'*

100. SIR ARTHUR MUNRO SUTHERLAND 1867-1953. SHIPOWNER

Often described as the last of Tyneside's merchant princes, Sir Arthur Munro Sutherland, a wealthy shipowner and public benefactor, never shone at school but was single-minded from the start. His grandfather had arrived in Newcastle on a sailing ship from Thurso, and his father became a provisions merchant and flour importer. At 16 Arthur became a junior clerk on Newcastle Quayside from which he came to dominate the North East shipping scene for many years. At 25 he purchased his first ship, a few years later the Sutherland Steam Shipping Company was established, and by the age of 45 he was a millionaire. Work for him had become a hobby (he never retired) and as an international figure in shipping and commerce, he was privileged to entertain royalty and statesmen. In the depth of the shipping depression of the 1930s his unbounded optimism, backed with orders for ships totalling over a million pounds, largely kept shipyards on the Tyne and Wear from closure.

As Sir Arthur made money he also gave chunks of it away to worthy causes in his native city. £100,000 was donated in the 1930s towards the cost of building the new medical school in Queen Victoria Road where his heraldic arms appear above the main entrance. The Newcastle Dental Hospital and School were also major recipients of his generosity and their former home in Northumberland Road is still known as the Sutherland Building. Newcastle Royal Grammar School, his old school, received liberal support as did many other local charities. After his death his Jesmond home, Thurso House, became the city's Mansion House, and Dunstanburgh Castle near Craster, which he also owned, was given to the nation.

Sir Arthur had inherited from his father an interest in civic affairs and ultimately became Sheriff, then Lord Mayor, and he remained an alderman until his death. Many honours came his way – he was knighted in 1920, created a baronet in 1921, received an honorary degree of Doctor of Civil Law and in 1943 became Sheriff of Northumberland.

101. FRANCES SWAN, 1829-1868. WIFE OF JOSEPH WILSON SWAN, INVENTOR OF THE INCANDESCENT ELECTRIC LAMP

Frances (Fanny) White was 33, a teacher and a friend of the John Mawson family, when she married Joseph Wilson Swan, Mawson's business partner in 1862. The Mawson Swan firm pio-

neered photography and at the time of his marriage Swan had also been experimenting with electric lamps. In 1867 John Mawson was killed in an explosion on the Town Moor (see page 26), and in January 1868 Fanny (right) died after giving birth to her third and fourth children, twin sons, who also died shortly afterwards. In 1871 Swan married Fanny's sister, Hannah, but they had to marry abroad as it was illegal at that time to marry a deceased wife's sister.

102. WILLIAM TOWARD, 1797-1865. MANUFACTURER OF STEAM ENGINES

His business was at Glasshouse Bridge Iron Works.

103. FREDERICK TURNBULL, 1868-1939. F.TURNBULL & CO., HEATON JUNCTION

The name may be seen on drain covers throughout Newcastle and the firm also made mining machinery and other castings. A blacksmith's son from Spennymoor, Fred Turnbull became a draughtsman engineer with a nearby firm, taking out a patent in 1895 for a friction clutch. A small legacy allowed him to travel in America after which he worked for Dorman Long in Middlesbrough and then set himself up in Newcastle as a consulting mining engineer. By 1910 he had premises at Heaton Junction, business prospered, and by the 1930s the Turnbull family could afford a house in Clayton Road, Jesmond. The iron foundry and engineering works remained a family business until the 1960s.

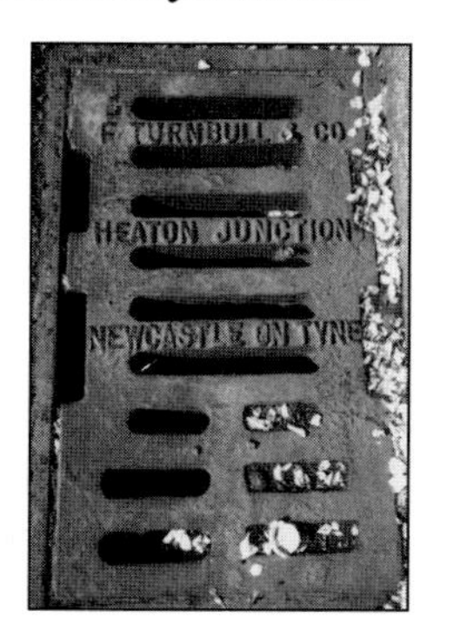

104. THOMAS HALL TWEEDY, 1816-1892. WOODCARVER AND GILDER

His premises were at Central Exchange Buildings in Grainger Street where painter Ralph Hedley was an apprentice. Central Exchange, intended by Richard Grainger to be a corn exchange (which the town refused) opened as a subscription news room in 1839. Following a serious fire in 1867 the news room eventually closed in 1870. Shortly afterwards, with T.P. Barkas, Tweedy successfully restored the waning fortunes of the Central Exchange by creating an art gallery open to all, though the introduction of lady members offended many older incumbents. Fire struck again in 1900 and the present shopping arcade was opened in 1906.

105. JOHN WATSON, 1784-1853

'These successively cut off in so brief a period were amongst the earliest victims of the pestilence [cholera] with which it pleased God to visit this town in 1853'. So reads the headstone for this family. John died 10th September aged 69, Barbara died 15th September aged 65 and Janet (daughter) died 12th September 1853 aged 26.

106. ROBERT SPENCE WATSON 1837-1911. SOLICITOR

Robert Spence Watson was said to have been the most powerful figure in Liberal politics outside of parliament, and the only Gateshead resident widely known beyond Tyneside.

Born in Gateshead, educated at the Quaker School at York, and University College London he qualified as a solicitor to join the family legal firm of Watson Booth founded by his father Joseph Watson. At the age of seven he had travelled with his father on the first train to make the through run from Gateshead to London.

At 26 Robert married Elizabeth Richardson, daughter of Edward Richardson who with his brother John ran a tannery and leather manufacturing business in Newcastle. The couple lived at Bensham Grove, Robert's family home (the house, on today's Bensham Bank, is marked by a plaque). Elizabeth too was a public figure with regard to women's education and suffrage, and it was to Bensham Grove that politicians, social reformers, poets, painters and European exiles flocked to seek friendship, help and advice.

Robert was involved in all aspects of education and was honorary secretary of the Literary and Philosophical Society in Newcastle before becoming its president in 1900. He travelled widely and nearly lost his life in France during the war with Prussia while distributing food to the starving peasants. He subsequently refused the offer of the French Legion of Honour. Robert became a Privy Councillor in 1907 and died four years later still living in the house where he was born.

INDEX TO NAMES, AND REFERENCE NUMBER